D0324090

THE CASE AGAINST
JOINING THE COMMON MARKET

By the same author

THE CASE AGAINST JOINING THE COMMON MARKET

PAUL EINZIG

MACMILLAN

ST MARTIN'S PRESS

© Paul Einzig 1971

First published 1971 by
MACMILLAN AND CO LTD
London and Basingstoke
Associated companies in New York Toronto
Dublin Melbourne Johannesburg and Madras

SBN 333 12639 4 (hard cover)

Printed in Great Britain by
R. & R. CLARK LTD
Edinburgh

Library of Congress catalog card no. 77–151309

Contents

Preface

ALTHOUGH I have always been vaguely opposed to joining the Common Market, until quite recently I did not feel sufficiently strongly about it to bring myself to contribute yet another book to the existing literature on that subject. My decision to interrupt my work on a highly technical book – even though I hope it will become my *magnum opus* – was triggered off mainly by my sudden realisation of the extent of the losses Britain would suffer by jettisoning the Commonwealth for the sake of joining the Common Market.

What made me realise it was the Australian Supplement published by *The Economist* on 22 August 1970, which states in its introductory article that Australia has the potentialities of a second United States. Exaggerated as this claim may appear at first sight, the contents of the Supplement amply confirm its substance if not perhaps its extent.

I could not resist writing to the Editor to ask him how anyone who has come to realise Australia's potentialities could want to dissociate Britain from that country for the sake of joining the Common Market. To my surprise *The Economist* published my letter. It was presumably in response to it that I received by air-mail a beautiful volume on New Zealand which made me realise how thoroughly English that lovely country is. It seems to me that to jettison it in order to earn our admission into the Common Market would be like handing over Cornwall to France as a price of her support of our application for membership.

There are other Commonwealth countries with which our close relationship is well worth retaining, even though others may be liabilities rather than assets. As far as Australia is concerned, her immense resources are only just beginning to be realised. If, instead of lending £500 million to enable an openly

hostile country, the Soviet Union, to become even more dangerous as a result of developing her industrial resources, we were
to employ the same amount for assisting Australia in the immense task of exploiting her mineral resources, the British nation
would stand a good chance of recovering a large part of its
former greatness through playing a leading part in the creation
of an English-speaking country of first-rate importance in the
Pacific, which would remain in close association with Britain.

'Will it be really worth Britain's while', I asked in my letter
to *The Economist*, 'to throw away her last chance of recovering
her national greatness by becoming the centre, or at any rate
one of the two leading members, of a Commonwealth which
would be treated on an equal footing by the present World
Powers? Is it really preferable to assume the Little Englander
role of an offshore island of Western Europe?'

Perhaps it is absurd that a naturalised British subject, brought
up on the Continent, who did not speak a word of English until
the age of twenty, should feel so strongly about the recovery of
Britain's lost national greatness and against reducing Britain to
the role of a member of an association of Continental nations.
When I was arguing the case against joining the Common
Market with a Scottish friend who was emphatically in favour
of joining, I suddenly came to realise the utter absurdity of the
situation. What right have I, who have been in this country for
a mere half-century, to argue about British national greatness
with one whose ancestors had presumably fought the Roman
legions at Hadrian's Wall? Yet I just cannot help feeling the
way in which I feel against adhering to the Treaty of Rome.

Nor am I too proud about fighting on the same side with
some of those who also oppose joining the Common Market.
Some of them are inspired by their dislike for the French, or by
their hatred of the Germans that has survived from two bitterly
fought world wars, or by their out-of-date feeling of superiority
over all Continental nations. On my part, I respect and admire
all nations of the Common Market. My culture is as much
French and German as English.

I have some hard things to say in this book about the French because of their short-sighted anti-American attitude, and because they are incapable of 'give and take'. I hate having to say these things because in spite of all, I do love the French. I am proud of my Sorbonne degree. I have works by scores of French authors – economists as well as literary supermen – on my bookshelves. It gives me great pleasure to hear French spoken with a Paris accent. And I cried on hearing the news of the fall of Paris in 1940. But I feel impelled to denounce France for pursuing a course that threatens to split the free world.

Although I have some hard things to say also about the United States, I feel much more closely related to English-speaking people all over the five continents than to Western European peoples. And I simply fail to understand men and women whose ancestors have lived on this island for a great many generations who feel enthusiasm bordering on fanaticism over a solution that would mean the end of hopes of recovering British national greatness, all for the sake of being admitted into an utterly undependable alliance which is liable to disintegrate at any moment.

How can they work up enthusiasm for a system under which the British taxpayer would contribute heavily to a common fund the operations of which would threaten to ruin highly efficient New Zealand food producers for the sake of subsidising inefficient French and German farmers? And how can they want to destroy deliberately what is left of Britain's special relationship with the United States – that special relationship which saved Britain in two world wars – for the sake of basing her very existence on the quicksands of the Common Market, some members of which are liable to break away, and even change sides, through domestic political developments?

I do not believe the Common Market has come to stay. It is liable to disintegrate for a wide variety of reasons discussed in Chapter 2. For the sake of becoming members during its brief existence Britain would lose the Commonwealth irretrievably, and the harm done to British–American relations might become irreparable.

This book is an eleventh-hour appeal to the British people

and their leaders to think again before committing Britain whether it would be really worth their while to make the sacrifices and take the grave risks involved, for the sake of the dubious results they hope to gain through joining the Common Market. The decision in October 1970 to impose duties on food imports constituted acceptance of the basic principle of the Common Agricultural Policy – an act of surrender before even the negotiations began properly. The decision to impose a duty on wheat and other land products imported from the United States even before we are forced to do so as a condition of our admission into the EEC was a free gift to American isolationists. It was the first shot fired in the coming trade war between Europe and the United States, which is bound to have disastrous financial, economic, political and military consequences. The new Government is well on its way towards sacrificing Britain's security based on the American nuclear deterrent, for the sake of flattering its way into the Common Market. But perhaps it is not too late to call a halt.

P. E.

120 CLIFFORD'S INN
LONDON, E.C.4
December 1970

CHAPTER ONE

From Hitler to Hallstein

THE origins of the plan of a united Western Europe have been variously traced back to *Pax Romana*, to Charlemagne, to the Hanseatic League, to Napoleon's Continental System, and to ideas of William Penn, Friedrich Naumann and Aristide Briand. My own theory is that the formula of a European Common Market, which is expected to lead to a complete economic and political integration of Western Europe, owes its origin, consciously or otherwise, to the short-lived practical experience in such integration between 1940 and 1944. The conquest of most of the Continent outside Russia by Hitler's armies in 1940 brought about a political and economic integration that came to be known under the name of Hitler's New Order in Europe. At a very early stage of its existence that system inspired an idea – *not* in Germany, let it be noted, but in Britain – that some such system should be made permanent regardless of the outcome of the war.

This idea found clear expression and support in an article by Mr C. W. Guillebaud in the December 1940 *Economic Journal* under the title of 'Hitler's New Economic Order in Europe'. It was the text of an address he delivered at the Royal Institute of International Affairs some three months after the conquest of Western Europe by Hitler was completed.

The chief originator of the scheme described by Guillebaud was Dr Walter Funk, Minister of National Economy of the Nazi Reich. To quote Guillebaud, Dr Funk offered a stable system of agricultural prices based on the high cost of production of inefficient European producers, '*insulated from the wide fluctuations of the world market, and divorced from the general level of prices at which food can be raised overseas with the aid of large-scale mechanised technique*' (my italics).

Guillebaud goes on:

> Whether the proposed economic policy for agriculture could succeed permanently is a matter of argument, but I do not think it could be ruled out of court as *prima facie* impossible, and if successful it would have much to commend it.

He adds that, even though the object of Funk's scheme was to ensure German supremacy, '*France . . . might stand to gain considerably in certain directions in the economic sphere*' (my italics).

In fairness to Guillabaud and to the Common Market, it is essential to quote the sentence that follows this remark:

> The Nazi scheme must be rejected, not on the ground that it is unworkable, nor that it is fundamentally unsound economically – parts of it may well come to be adopted later in a modified form – but because it is based on a one-sided German hegemony over the whole continent of Europe, which would be unendurable; the price to be paid for such merits as it possesses would be far too high and, moreover, there are grave economic defects which have to be set against these merits.

Nevertheless, Guillebaud continues:

> Nature and geographical facts have placed Germany in the centre of the great area. . . . The great task of statesmanship after the war will be to secure the willing cooperation of Germany in the economic reconstruction of Europe on the basis of the rights and interests of all the peoples involved.

In other words, Guillebaud advocated Hitler's New Economic Order without Hitler. In 1940–41 I strongly criticised his idea in the *Economic Journal*, in *Time and Tide*, in the *Financial News* and in my book *Appeasement Before, During and After the War*, mainly because of the unfortunate timing of its publication. Hitler was at the height of his power and Britain was fighting him single-handed. Whether the creation of a European Common Market without Hitler would be a good thing or not appeared to be at the time a question of purely academic interest. But publicising in 1940 British advocacy of perpetuating the main principle of Hitler's New Order was inexpedient. It was liable to encourage *collaborateurs* in occupied Europe to the utmost, at the same time as discouraging Britain's only fighting allies, the resistance movements.

For this reason, I attacked Guillebaud for all I was worth. I may have been grossly unfair to him, for he proved to have been right in envisaging the possibility of the operation of the New Order with the participation of a de-Hitlerised Germany. But he was right at the wrong moment and for the wrong reason. For had Germany not attacked Soviet Russia and had Japan not attacked the United States – both events were quite impossible to foresee in 1940 – Hitler's New Order would not have assumed the form of a European Common Market created by common consent but would have been imposed on conquered Europe by Hitler, irrespective of whether Guillebaud and the rest of us outside Germany considered it 'unendurable'.

Guillebaud was by no means alone in favouring the New Order at a time when the chances of its creation by anyone but Hitler appeared to be negligible. Keynes himself was inclined to give it sympathetic consideration, judging by the following passage from his letter to me, dated 8 January 1941:

> Not all would agree with him [Guillebaud] but a great many would, and I am sure this is a view . . . which deserves ventilation. We shall make a bad peace if we disregard the sort of things which Guillebaud is emphasising.

On the basis of the above evidence I feel justified in describing the Common Market – the economic integration of the Continent, based on Professor Hallstein's Common Agricultural Policy – as an idea inherited from the Hitler regime. Of course this fact by itself would not justify its rejection. But it is a matter of historic truth which should be placed on record, if only to prove that the Common Market can have no pride of ancestry. What is more important, has it any hope of posterity? It was conceived with evil intent. Its original idea of achieving through its application the domination of Europe by a totalitarian

Power has been abandoned, even though two of the participants in the EEC do entertain hopes of achieving some degree of hegemony through its application. And it is my contention that its present declared purpose is, in a different sense, just as dangerous as the Hitler–Funk idea of using the original version of the Common Market scheme for the perpetual oppression of Europe.

This may sound absurd. Hallstein and others who have been making superhuman efforts to overcome the innumerable obstacles to the creation of a united Europe are idealist visionaries as far as Europe is concerned. But they cannot see, or refuse to see, beyond the confines of Europe.

Guillebaud makes it abundantly clear that the system of European economic integration – whether in Hitler's New Order or in Hallstein's Common Market vaguely foreshadowed by Guillebaud in its broad outlines – must be built round the policy of maintaining the prices of European land products well above their world prices. This end is now sought to be achieved by means of customs barriers against agricultural imports from other continents and by means of buying up surplus products that would tend to depress their prices. The first device deprives more efficient producers in other continents of their natural markets in Europe, which is bad enough. But to make matters much worse, the surplus products to be bought up by the Common Market authorities will be dumped on the world market.

Since artificially high prices in Europe will stimulate production, in given circumstances the dumping of certain products is liable to assume appreciable dimensions. The standard of living of food producers in other continents will be reduced artificially for the sake of raising the standard of living of European food producers. This goes far beyond anything Funk had in mind when he first put forward the idea of a European New Economic Order. This aspect of the Common Market is so inherently destructive that it could out-Hitler even Hitler in its results – though, in all probability, had Hitler remained in power he would have discovered in due course the damaging effects which the application of the Funk formula could cause outside Europe.

Even in its modified form and under the guidance of statesmen who have nothing in common with Hitler and Funk, the Common Agricultural Policy has succeeded in dividing free Europe into two camps, and its extended application, by leading to a trade war, is liable to split the free world. The resulting destructive economic, social and political consequences would prove the Common Agricultural Policy well worthy of its originator. It would be comic if it were not so tragic that the Communist bloc alone would stand to benefit by the posthumous application of Hitler's agricultural system.

It is mainly this aspect of the New Order in Europe, inherited by Hallstein from Hitler, that has been all along the main obstacle to Britain's participation in the Common Market. But for the determination of the EEC to aim at food prices well above the world level, a free trade area on the lines of EFTA, within which customs barriers for industrial goods would be removed, might have been in operation throughout Western Europe for many years. This has been all the time the British idea of close co-operation between countries on this side of the Iron Curtain. It has been mainly the difficulties and complications arising from the fundamental aim of the Common Market to bolster up food prices at an artificially high level that has prevented Britain from adhering to the Treaty of Rome.

There is, of course, an unanswerable case for keeping agriculture in Britain and in Europe alive in spite of the higher cost of production compared with agriculture working with lower production costs outside Europe. But there is no reason why each Government should not solve this domestic problem in accordance with its special requirements. The British formula of subsidising domestic agricultural producers was rejected by the authors and executors of the Treaty of Rome who preferred to follow the Funk formula. It is immaterial whether or not those who negotiated and drafted the Treaty of Rome and those who apply its terms to the EEC and want to force them on Britain are aware of this. The inescapable fact is that it was the

basic idea inherited from Hitler's Third Reich that was, and
still is at the time of writing, responsible for splitting Western
Europe into two economic camps.

Admittedly there were, and still are, other major points of
disagreement. But as far as Britain is concerned the agricultural
aspects of the Funk Plan, and the effect of their application to
the Commonwealth, is the principal obstacle. Were it not for
the determination with which the Common Market seeks
to apply Hitler's New Economic Order in the agricultural
sphere, a compromise would have been reached many years
ago.

It is true, the present version of the New Economic Order in
Europe no longer serves the purpose of consolidating German
hegemony over the Continent. In the meantime the balance of
power has changed as a result of the division of Germany and
as a result of France's remarkable recovery under the de Gaulle
regime. The two leading Western European Powers have to rule
jointly, but they have chosen to do so on the basis of the main
principle of the Funk agricultural policy.

The British negotiators, whether Conservative or Socialist,
would have to accept that unpalatable policy if they wanted to
come to terms with the EEC. They aimed, and are still aiming,
at securing concessions to mitigate its impact on British agriculture and the British cost of living, and on the Commonwealth
countries which are likely to be affected to the highest degree.
It remains to be seen whether the EEC will be prepared to go
far enough to meet the British demands for concessions. If the
negotiations resumed by the new Conservative Government in
1970 should break down, it would be due in all probability to
failure to reach an agreement on the application of the basic
principle of Hitler's New Economic Order in Europe.

Were it not for that principle, closer economic collaboration
between the countries of Western Europe would indeed be a
welcome development. Although, as the following chapters will
try to prove, in any case there must necessarily be many 'ifs' and
'buts' to be overcome – and there are many basic disadvantages to face – but for the Common Agricultural Policy there

would be no unsurmountable obstacle to the achievement of a high degree of economic unity between Britain and the EEC.

Throughout the negotiations that have been proceeding off and on – more off than on – ever since 1962, the policy of dear food and the effect of Funk's formula on Commonwealth relations have been the main stumbling-block. No advantages that could reasonably be expected from joining the Common Market would be sufficient to compensate Britain for giving way on these two points, especially as the Common Agricultural Policy would be also inevitably detrimental to Britain's relations with the United States.

Apart altogether from the problem of agricultural integration and its implications, it is doubtful whether Britain could expect a net advantage from joining the Common Market. Chapter 2 will try to prove that from a politico-military point of view the balance of arguments is distinctly against a coalition which, under French inspiration, is directed largely against continued American military presence in Europe. I shall also argue that the Common Market, having 'no pride of ancestry', has 'no hope of posterity', because for political reasons Britain could not depend on the lasting character of the EEC. The next chapter seeks to discredit the widely held belief that 'the more we are together, the happier we shall be' – that economic integration would necessarily create and maintain a friendly atmosphere between the nations of Western Europe. Quite possibly, indeed probably, the manifold conflicts of interest between them will act as constant irritants and are liable to culminate in a disintegration of the Common Market amidst circumstances that would leave much ill-feeling behind between the former partners.

So much for the political aspects of the subject. Turning to its economic aspects, Chapter 4 denounces the gross exaggeration of the extent to which an extension of the size of a market is claimed to determine the degree of prosperity within the market. In this respect, as in several other respects, this book challenges dogmas that have been accepted almost uncritically by British opinion for a very long time. Another of these dogmas is that an increase in the size of firms or combines that would be assisted by joining the Common Market would be an unqualified advantage. That argument is dealt with in Chapter 5 which points out that the EEC itself is in two minds whether to encourage or discourage amalgamations that would lead to the creation of super-combines comparable in size to their rivals in the United States.

Chapter 6 expresses doubt about the extent to which joining the Common Market would necessarily make a fundamental difference to the extent of competition. It also challenges the dogmatic belief in the all-curing effect of unlimited competition, belief which has secured many adherents in this country for the movement favouring Britain's adhesion to the Common Market. Expression of dissent from such a widely accepted view – it is held unanimously among Liberals and almost unanimously among Conservatives – is bound to be unpopular. Likewise, Chapter 7, criticising the all-too-prevalent growth-hysteria at the same time as expressing doubts as to whether joining the EEC would necessarily accelerate our rate of growth, is yet another exercise in 'the gentle art of making enemies'.

The next chapter examines the all-important question whether Britain could find a lasting solution for her balance of payments problem by joining the Common Market. It arrives at the conclusion that, unless the British worker could be induced to work harder and strike less, membership in the EEC is liable to be a disadvantage from the point of view of the balance of payments. This would be especially so if willingness of the other EEC countries to allow Britain to run up short-term liabilities were to reduce the incentive for Britain to work out her own salvation through her increased exertions and through practising self-restraint. The effect of joining the Common Market on the extent of the 'English disease' in this country and abroad is discussed in Chapter 9.

Chapter 10 examines the arguments in favour of joining the Common Market for the sake of the freedom of movement of labour and of capital across the borders of the member countries.

FROM HITLER TO HALLSTEIN

The advantages such freedom is claimed to convey are examined critically.

Monetary unification is held out as an attraction for the sake of which it would be well worth our while to join the EEC. Chapter 11 describes the difficulties to be encountered at the various stages through which it could be achieved. It warns that monetary integration could only be completed at the price of giving up a considerable part of national sovereignty. There could be no unified currency without a central authority which would take no orders from national Governments, Parliaments and electorates. Economic integration, and even political integration, would have to proceed very far before genuine monetary integration became feasible.

Having discussed the claims of various alleged advantages Britain was supposed to derive through joining the EEC, Chapter 12 and the three following chapters examine the main objections to the policy of economic integration in Western Europe. Even allowing for the fact that, while some of the sacrifices involved in joining the EEC are obvious and to some extent quantifiable, the advantages claimed for it are vague and difficult to prove, the conclusion that the disadvantages would greatly outweigh the advantages seems to be inescapable. One of these costs which even the most enthusiastic supporters of the Common Market policy admit is the inevitable effect on prices in Britain, discussed in Chapter 13. The cost of living and the cost of production would be affected as a result of the substantial increase in food prices caused by the application of the Common Agricultural Policy and as a result of the adoption of the value-added tax.

I attach particular importance to Chapter 14 which deals with the effect of joining the Common Market on Britain's relations with the Commonwealth. As I have already said in the Preface, it was mainly the full realisation of what Britain stands to lose by abandoning her special economic relationship with countries such as Australia and New Zealand – to mention only these two – that induced me to produce the present indictment of the policy to jettison loyal British countries for the sake of establishing precarious relationships with undependable Western European countries.

Hardly less important is the disadvantage, discussed in Chapter 15, of driving the United States into adopting a policy of isolation by throwing in our lot with France in her present anti-American mood and with other Western European countries largely under her influence. Both our security and our prosperity depend very largely on our friendship with the United States.

Chapter 16 deals with the possibility that Britain might be unable to join the Common Market because the terms on which she would be admitted would be unacceptable. It warns against unduly prolonged negotiations as a result of which Britain might get the worst of every possible world, because her present trading partners might complete other arrangements in other directions, in the expectation that Britain would abandon them.

The concluding chapter suggests alternatives to joining the Common Market. We might carry on as we are, making the best possible use of our membership in EFTA and of Commonwealth Preference. We might try to persuade the Commonwealth to join EFTA as full members or as associates, and we should do our best to strengthen our association especially with Australia, New Zealand and Canada. We could try to persuade the United States and Canada to join a North Atlantic Free Trade Association (NAFTA) and invite other Commonwealth countries and countries such as Japan to join it. Finally we could aim at a much more ambitious organisation – a Free World Free Trade Association.

I have no illusions about the difficulties of arriving at any of these solutions, or about the disadvantages of all of them, similar in many respects to the disadvantages of joining the Common Market. But I feel that to revive the Commonwealth or to unite all English-speaking countries in a free trade area is an aim for which it would be well worth while to make some sacrifices.

What matters is that British negotiators and British public opinion should not allow itself to be hypnotised by the oft-repeated contention that Britain's choice lies between joining the Common Market and declining into insignificance. Lack of adequate realisation that alternative solutions do exist is weakening our bargaining position at the same time as encouraging the EEC to drive the hardest possible bargain. It is of the utmost importance that we, and they too, should realise the existence of practicable and in many ways preferable alternative solutions. British public opinion and political opinion should not be misled by propaganda minimising the disadvantages of joining the Common Market and exaggerating its advantages. Even if we were to decide to join we should at least do so with our eyes wide open.

CHAPTER TWO

Political and Military Aspects

BEFORE examining the economic arguments for and against joining the Common Market, it is necessary to deal with the political and military arguments. For many people who are not enthusiastic about the economic case for joining it, and even some who would be decidedly against joining it on purely economic grounds, are willing to pay the price in terms of economic disadvantages for the sake of the advantages they believe it offers in the sphere of international politics and in the military sphere.

There are people who realise and deplore the decline of Britain's political influence in world affairs and of her military power, but deem it inconceivable to 'put the clock back' by trying to regain a large part of her former armed strength and political influence. Indeed the trend is still in the direction of further disarmament, although this inevitably means a further decline in Britain's prestige and influence in world affairs. But advocates of the Common Market solution hope that we might eat our cake and keep at least some of it by joining our remaining forces with those of the Six of Western Europe and that our combined military power could secure political influence for us as partners in the Common Market.

Those who argue on these lines hope that the EEC, enlarged by the entry of Britain and a few smaller Western European countries, would create a 'third force' between the two World Powers, the United States and the U.S.S.R. (In a few years they will have to think in terms of a 'fourth force' when China will rise to equality or near-equality with the two giant Powers.) They feel this 'third force' might hold the balance between the major opponents and could use its power in the interests of peace. Individually Britain, or France, or West Germany, are unable to exert much influence. But, it is argued, the combined strength of virtually the entire continent on this side of the Iron Curtain could not be disregarded even if it could not expect to be treated on an equal footing with the World Powers.

The answer to this argument is that it would be morally wrong to aim at holding the balance between good and evil, and that it would be politically wrong to aim at being neutral between Imperialist Soviet Russia or Imperialist Communist China and the only country capable of frustrating their ambition of world conquest. The vital interests of Western Europe are identical with those of the United States – to help the free world to safeguard its freedom. Whatever anti-Americans in France or in other countries say about the United States, they cannot honestly suspect her of trying to conquer free countries either through invasion or through subversion. The United States may aim at achieving political influence to ensure the co-operation of other free countries in her stand against those who threaten their freedom. She may aim at buying up European industries and financing the purchases with the aid of money borrowed in Europe, an effort which is liable to cause resentment. But let us just try to compare this political influence and this 'economic invasion' with the military invasion and conquest of Hungary and of Czechoslovakia by Soviet Russia, or with the military invasion and conquest of Tibet by China. No freedom-loving country can possibly hesitate as to which is preferable.

Admittedly, it is to the interests of the United States and of the entire free world that Western Europe should be strong and united. But from a purely political and military point of view there is nothing that NATO could not do a great deal better than even an enlarged EEC could possibly hope to do. For NATO represents the combined forces of non-Communist and non-neutral Europe – with the notable and deplorable absence of France – *plus* the forces of North America and Canada.

France has withdrawn from NATO and is pursuing independent and even anti-European political and military policies, on the sole ground that NATO is dominated by the United States. But the American answer to that problem is 'No representation without taxation' – in other words, France and the other Western European countries could have increased and could still increase their relative influence in NATO by increasing the relative strength of their armed forces. It is extremely short-sighted – and also short-memoried – on the part of France to adopt and maintain her 'Yankee go home' attitude, considering the difficulty she experienced in both world wars in inducing the United States to abandon her isolationist attitude. M. Pompidou should re-read M. Reynaud's pathetic appeal to Roosevelt from Bordeaux. Does he want to risk having to make a similar appeal?

The origin of this anti-American policy of France lies in the anti-de Gaulle attitude of President Roosevelt. Because General de Gaulle was incapable of forgetting and forgiving slights to which he was subjected more than a quarter of a century ago, he was prepared to risk the security of his country and of the free world by splitting the united defensive forces against Communist aggression. His successors might learn sooner or later that it is much easier to send the Yankees home than to induce them to return to Europe when they are once more needed here desperately.

Admittedly, American greed in trying to grasp all French and Western European industries worth having has contributed towards the French anti-American attitude which survived de Gaulle's departure. But there could have been, and could still be, other devices to check the 'economic invasion' in so far as it is unwelcome, without having to split the free world to achieve that end.

Should, as a result of anti-Americanism in Europe, isolationism gain the upper hand in the United States Congress and in American public opinion – and the French attitude goes a long way towards producing precisely that result – no amount of pooling of Western European economic and military resources could compensate us for the withdrawal of the American forces, actual and potential, from NATO. If Britain's entry into the EEC should lead Washington to the conclusion that Western Europe should now stand on its own legs, the barest possibility of the resulting disengagement would be an unanswerable argument against joining the EEC.

There is another almost equally strong political argument against it. The only really good thing that has emerged from the Second World War has been that, after many centuries of enmity, France and Germany have discovered that they could and should live together on friendly terms. This change was not the result of Western European economic integration. It predates the Treaty of Rome and predates considerably the implementation of that Treaty. In fact, there were moments during the 'sixties when conflicting economic interests arising from the application of the Treaty of Rome put the newly-established political friendship of the two principal Continental Powers of Western Europe to a very severe test. There is, moreover, a degree of rivalry between them for supremacy within the EEC that is liable to endanger their newly-found friendship.

The question is, how would Britain's adhesion to the Common Market affect the precariously balanced Franco-German relationship? As one of the three leading members of the enlarged EEC, Britain would have to side with either the one or with the other on many occasions when they disagree on some major issue. Each would do its utmost to enlist Britain's support. At present France, with her superior military strength, and Germany, with her superior economic strength, maintain equilibrium within the EEC, equilibrium which might well become upset with Britain's entry. Or possibly friendly relations between the two leading Continental Powers would be strengthened by France and Germany joining forces to oppose our interests and settling their differences by gaining advantages at our expense. Inevitable intrigues between the British–French–German triangle would endanger unity within the EEC.

The permanent unity of Western Europe cannot be taken for granted. France is inclined to withdraw from the activities of the EEC whenever she cannot have her way. Some day she might withdraw completely, in the same way as she has withdrawn from NATO and from other inter-Allied arrangements. If she did that it would effectively break up the EEC, and well she knows it. Hence the brinkmanship with which she often succeeds in imposing her will on her five partners in the EEC. Another perturbing possibility is that a General Election might well bring to power a Communist-inspired Left-wing Government. This might easily happen also in Italy.

Likewise, the possibility that West Germany might be unable to resist the temptation to sever or loosen her commitments with the West for the sake of being able to achieve some degree of reunification with East Germany should not be ignored. The political and economic consequences of such a change would be very grave and must be taken into consideration before deciding whether to join the EEC.

How would it affect the political outlook for the Common Market if Britain joined it? Should British membership in the Common Market be able to prevent a Communist victory at a General Election in France or Italy, or a West German–Soviet *rapprochement*? If not, the whole exercise would cease to be able to serve its main political object, which is to contain Communist-Imperialist expansion. It would definitely lead the United States towards the conclusion that it is not worth while to try to defend the European continent against the Communist menace.

Should such a situation arise, the question that would matter more than any other from the point of view of Britain's chances of survival is whether the United States would write her off as well as the rest of Europe and would base her defensive strategy on long-range missiles and nuclear submarines without wanting to maintain costly and vulnerable bases on this side of the Atlantic. The answer would be inevitably influenced by Britain's decision whether to join the Common Market. Should she become an integral part of the EEC, and should French anti-Americanism gain the upper hand, there would be a strong inclination in Washington to leave Britain to her fate together with the rest of Western Europe. But if Britain should choose to rely on NATO rather than on the EEC, and more especially, if she were to try to strengthen her link with the United States by favouring the establishment of a North Atlantic Free Trade Association (NAFTA), the United States would be much more likely to retain the American military bases in the U.K.

Joining the EEC might well lead to the political and military isolation of Britain if one or more of the main continental member States should turn leftwards, or if they should be over-run by the U.S.S.R. as they were by Germany in 1940. She could not even rely upon the highly valuable support she received from the Commonwealth in two world wars if she severed her trade links with them. Even if all economic considerations were in favour of joining the Common Market, surely considerations of national security, indeed of national survival, would have to take precedence over mere considerations of prosperity. Freedom from fear is even more important than freedom from want.

Possibly in face of the common danger the United States might decide to retain the British bases regardless of our membership in the EEC which, even in the absence of a drift towards Communism of some of its members, might tend to be anti-American under French influence. It is one thing to rely on American support when the Americans are on the spot, and quite another thing to induce them to return to Europe once 'Yankee go home' pressure has succeeded in inducing them to leave us to our own devices. Experience of both world wars proved how extremely difficult it is to induce the United States to overcome isolationism. So why encourage American isolationism by joining the Common Market?

Another aspect of the problem is that should, contrary to all my expectations, Britain's admission to the Common Market increase her economic strength, her gain would be, to a large degree, the loss of the United States. American opinion is beginning to realise this. Until some years ago it was decidedly in favour of strengthening the EEC by persuading Britain to join it, as a means of reducing the burden and responsibility of keeping Western Europe free of Communism. But now, in the absence of a military attack, Western Europe is sufficiently prosperous to resist Communist peaceful penetration if its peoples want to do so. Americans are beginning to feel it is time for them to concentrate on safeguarding their own financial interests and to let Europe take care of itself. And should the success of an enlarged EEC mean substantial losses of markets for American exports, it might strengthen pressure on the Administration in favour of a complete withdrawal from Europe, including Britain.

From the point of view of national security and, indeed, of national survival, it would be a fatal mistake to make Britain dependent on Western Europe to too high a degree. Integration with Western Europe might mean a degree of inter-European division of labour which would deprive Britain of arms and essential civilian supplies as a result of another enemy occupation of the Continent. It would take time before the supplies for which we would come to depend on Western Europe could be replaced from overseas, and in the next war there might not be enough time available for it.

Looking further ahead, it is necessary to envisage a situation in which the main potential enemy would be not the Soviet Union but China. Owing to the numerical superiority of the Chinese people, it would take the combined military strength of Russia, the United States and Western Europe to contain its Imperialist expansion in Asia and elsewhere. From that point of view the decision of the Soviet Union whether to be in the first place Communist or Russian will largely depend on the combined strength of the West. Moscow would never risk an open alliance with an isolated Western Europe as a deterrent to Chinese Communist Imperialism. But it might risk it if the Western European forces were part of the much larger total Western forces. From the point of view of avoiding a war with China it would therefore be a grave mistake to divide the Western forces by substituting for NATO a military power that would consist exclusively of Western European forces without any really effective nuclear deterrent.

It is even more important, especially during the 'seventies before China becomes more dangerous than Soviet Russia, to avoid creating a situation in which the Soviet Government might feel tempted to attempt to expand sufficiently to be able to face China later on an equal footing. So long as an invasion of Western Europe would mean a clash with the United States, the Soviet Union would not risk it, as even a victory would weaken it to such an extent as to be unable to face China's increased power. But a withdrawal of American forces from Europe would open for Soviet Russia the possibility of a relatively easy conquest of Western Europe, which would be followed by her expansion to the Middle East and India. The Kremlin might assume that once Western Europe and Southern Asia is under its overlordship, its would be able to face China on terms equal even after the latter has completed her industrialisation and has increased her military striking power.

The continued presence of American forces in Europe and in the Mediterranean would alone be sufficient deterrent against Moscow risking such an ambitious adventure. If by the time China becomes ready to embark on a policy of aggression Western Europe, the Middle East and Southern Asia still retain their freedom thanks to the American presence, the Kremlin might be inclined to think in terms of associating with the free world to offset the weight of China's power. But a withdrawal of the American forces as a result of the short-sighted French policy imposed on the EEC as a whole, and their withdrawal from Britain as a result of her adhesion to the anti-American Common Market, would be likely to induce Soviet Russia to aggrandise herself at our expense before China comes to represent an acute menace.

For this reason alone, Britain should keep out of the EEC, at least until France discards her anti-American attitude and returns to NATO. It was a grave error even to initiate negotiations to enter the EEC until France has returned to her former allies by rejoining NATO instead of taking an independent line in her foreign and military policy. Thus, so far from strengthening the case for Britain's adhesion to the Common Market, in existing circumstances political and military considerations should in themselves be more than sufficient to tip the balance of arguments against it. A split in the Western camp between the United States and Western Europe and an encouragement of American isolationism by the EEC that included Britain would be fatal from the point of view of the defences of Britain and of the entire free world.

CHAPTER THREE

'The More We Are Together . . .'

ONE of the main non-economic arguments in favour of Western European economic integration is that it tends to bring about closer political relationships between the nations included in the Common Market. From the point of view of the political power and influence of the EEC it would be of immense advantage if, as a result of their economic integration, the member countries were to be welded together into a European United States, the component parts of which would be as closely related to each other as the North American States that form the United States of America.

For a great many people in Britain this argument alone would be sufficient to reject the whole idea of joining the EEC. They want to remain purely British and are firmly opposed to re-linquishing any essential part of their country's absolute sovereignty. Their feelings may be respected without sharing them. If it appeared to be likely that genuine and lasting political integration would be brought about by the success of the attempt at economic integration through the Common Market experiment, Britain would be faced with a dilemma whether it would be worth her while, for the sake of such prospects, to give up all hope of recovering British national greatness with the aid of a restoration of closer relations with the loyal countries of the Commonwealth.

But the dilemma does not arise. For it seems certain that the principle of 'The more we are together, the happier we shall be' does not apply as a rule to relationships between nations. Of course it would be a good thing if the nations were to get to know each other better. There should be a great deal of inter-change in every sphere between them. Nations could and should absorb small proportions of each others' nationals. They should pool their culture and their civilisation for the benefit of the general progress of mankind. They should exchange their technical know-how. They should learn each others' languages, each others' history. They should exchange students; they should spend holidays abroad; they should attend international conferences and festivals of every kind. But they should not aim at merging into each other even if this were possible.

There are many historical instances of nations and races losing their identities as a result of conquering or being conquered. Possibly after a more or less long period the nations that have been merged might come to forget their separate identities and to feel like one nation. But this might take centuries, and the process might never be complete. It became complete between the conquered English and the conquering Normans, but it has never become complete between the English people on the one hand and the Welsh people, the Scottish people or the Irish people on the other, in spite of having lived together for many centuries.

It seems utterly unlikely that a high degree of integration could be brought about between modern race-conscious nations living on separate clearly defined territories, even if it were possible to elaborate and apply an economic system under which they would come to regard their economic interests as identical. The comparison with the experience of the United States is utterly false. It is true, the United States, having been originally mainly of English descent and traditions, is now a melting-pot in which nationals and races from all over the world have merged into a single nation. But this result might not have ever been achieved if the immigrants from various countries lived on separate territories from the very outset. Although there are colonies of various nationals and races in New York and in other cities, they gradually merge into each other, and people of the second generation consider themselves just Americans. Most immigrants go to the United States with the intention of merging into the American nation.

But is it conceivable that children born since the Treaty of

Rome, or after its implementation, would ever come to consider themselves simply Europeans and not Frenchmen, Germans, Italians, etc.? Living as they do on their respective national territories, they will never merge into a European nation comparable with the American nation. They will retain their separate languages, their national characteristics, their national culture. They will never identify themselves with a United States of Europe to anything like the extent to which the various races and the individual States in the United States identify themselves with the United States.

Even if the economic interests of the nations linked with each other under the Treaty of Rome were not only identical but were seen to be identical by all concerned, the process of political integration beyond the status of an alliance, or at most some loose form of limited confederation, would be a slow one. And the economic interests of the nations that are joined together by the EEC, or will join that group of countries later, is very far from being identical. Nor is there any reason for expecting that the existing conflicts of national interest in Western Europe could ever be smoothed out completely by any process of further economic, legal, cultural, social and political integration.

Of course conflicts of interests necessarily arise even within every individual country. They exist between various social classes, between races, between various geographical districts, between various occupations, between age groups, etc. But all those who represent these conflicting interests belong to the same State, they are subject to the same constitutional and legal system. In democratic countries they have a chance at elections to determine their destinies. Anyhow they take it for granted that they belong together for better or for worse. Admittedly, more or less everybody is more or less dissatisfied with the Government of the day (‘It is raining, damn the Government’ is an Italian saying), with the operation of the political system and with the working of the national economy. But their dissatisfaction seldom rises to a level at which a sufficient number of people would come to feel it imperative to disrupt the unity of the State to be able to do that.

CM B

The situation is totally different if the unpopular measures or disadvantages imposed on a large section of the nations within the EEC were imposed on them not by their own Government but by some international authority. Then measures which are considered intolerable are liable to generate a strong and growing feeling that the system under which such measures or disadvantages are forced on them should be terminated through breaking away from the international organisation. This could be done incomparably more easily than breaking up an established national State. Realisation of the possibility of bringing major disadvantages to an end by leaving the EEC would tend to generate and strengthen pressure on the Governments of disaffected peoples to do so. It would be supported by many who would not think of advocating or approving of a policy or action aimed at the disruption of the national State. But in the EEC there is always bound to be a feeling that the remedy for some trouble caused by an unpopular measure lies in the hands of the member countries.

Economic integration which is not preceded by safely established political integration rests on very unstable foundations. It is liable to be disrupted as a result of a change of Government or of a General Election in any of the major member countries, or even by violent street disturbances forcing the hands of the Government in office. Dissatisfaction is liable to arise through conflicts between vital interests of the member nations, even though the cracks of disagreements can be temporarily papered over as a result of political compromises. They can be imposed on the nations by the central administrative body of the EEC if it is given the required authority to do so. A Government which is strongly nationalistic – such as the de Gaulle regime had been – or which is not sufficiently strong to withstand pressures by interests affected adversely by the operation of the Common Market, is liable to disregard major long-range interests of closer integration and break away from its association with other States.

As a result of such conflicts of interests France repeatedly withdrew from the activities of the EEC to a varying extent.

Admittedly, each time she returned eventually to the fold – usually after her claims were met more or less. But some day she might withdraw altogether. Being the most difficult partner among the Six, she has to be humoured by making her concessions at the expense of the other partners, or to the detriment of the progress towards integration. Some day the concession granted to her might be found by some other member country too costly and too much against its vital interests, in which case it would be the turn of the Government concerned to play brinkmanship or even to break away well and truly.

What matters is to realise that the assumption that progress towards economic integration necessarily means harmonious co-existence of the nations within the Common Market is entirely unjustified. Quite on the contrary, the Common Market increases the likelihood of sharp disagreements based on conflict of interests between the nations tied together in an uneasy partnership. Admittedly, conflicts of interest arise also between nations which have no ties with each other, and the settlement of difference between their Governments, or the breakdown of the attempts to settle them, often leaves bitter feelings of resentment behind. But the scope for disagreement is widened considerably within an association of nations such as the Common Market, because of the increase in the number of spheres in which policies and decisions are apt to encroach upon the preserves of national interests. For instance, although the cost of living of independent countries is influenced by policies and actions of other countries, that influence is indirect and far from obvious. On the other hand, the cost of living of member countries in the Common Market, and more especially the cost of living of new entrants, is affected by the policies of the Common Market much more directly and to a much higher degree.

This alone would be sufficient to generate ill-feeling among the people who have to pay higher prices. More will be said about this in Chapter 13. Here we are concerned with the subject solely from the point of view of refuting the contention that 'the more we are together, the happier we shall be'. It is one thing to import inflation from other countries, or to suffer a rise in the prices of imported goods through changes of parities or through international influences for which no country can be blamed. It is quite a different thing to experience a sharp rise in our cost of living as a direct and obvious result of becoming associated with other nations, brought about by deliberate action for the sake of being permitted to become associated with them. Each time a housewife has to pay higher prices for her purchases she will have a sense of grievance against the countries for whose benefit our prices would be made to rise.

This is only one of the innumerable causes of resentment which is bound to arise between the nations belonging to an economic union, not only at the moment when they pay the immediate price of their admission but, to a smaller degree, throughout their membership in that union. The EEC interferes with the economies of member countries in so many directions that its interference is liable to hurt essential national interests in a wide variety of ways. This argument alone would not necessarily dispose of the case for joining the Common Market. Those in favour of it argue that the economic advantages derived from joining it, though less obvious than its economic disadvantages, would outweigh the latter in the long run. We shall examine that argument in detail in later chapters. What matters is that it is entirely mistaken to expect adhesion to the EEC to create a brotherly feeling among member nations, such as exists within a nation or even within a long-established federation of nations. Whatever conclusions we may derive about the case for joining the EEC purely for the sake of the economic advantages expected from membership in it, the argument that it would create closer political and human sympathies between member nations, and that it would therefore strengthen thereby their united political and military front, is untenable.

Progress towards closer economic integration within the EEC, which has been proceeding ever since its creation, creates very much additional potential cause for resentment by the nations which feel they have been victimised and have been made to pay a disproportionately high price for satisfying the interests of other member nations. Indeed it is little short of a miracle that the EEC has succeeded so far in surviving the various major clashes between Governments and the chronic resentment within particular member countries. But the twelve years that elapsed have not provided a reliable test for the possibility of a permanent survival of the EEC notwithstanding inner conflicts and dissatisfaction. Although the twelve years were punctuated by major crises – some of which brought the EEC to the verge of disintegration – the EEC survived because of circumstances which cannot be assumed to remain perpetual.

Foremost among these circumstances has been the degree of political stability in France under General de Gaulle's quasi-dictatorship. Even after his resignation the Gaullist Party re-mained in control and his successor, M. Pompidou, has been able to prevent, up to the time of writing, a relapse of France into the chronic political chaos from which de Gaulle had rescued her. Since the ruler of France was prepared to remain within the EEC – at a price – ill-feeling over real or imagined grievances among various sections of the French people was unable to force the French Government to break away.

West Germany felt impelled to remain within the EEC, be-cause of the apparent hopelessness of German reunification. Both France and Germany entertained hopes of achieving un-disputed supremacy over the Common Market, hopes that would vanish if Britain joined it, because the weaker side would expect to be supported by Britain against the stronger side. Meanwhile, although there is no sign of the former enmity be-tween the two leading continental countries, there is very little love lost between the two peoples, and the flare-up of economic disagreements does not exactly help towards increasing its extent.

There is an ever-present possibility that discontented ele-ments in any one of the major member countries might gain the upper hand and force their Government either to make impossible demands or to leave the EEC. In this respect post-de Gaulle France is the chief danger spot. Throughout the de

Gaulle regime, and even after the General's departure, she has been taking an independent line in economic as well as political spheres. Her partners found on many occasions that their choice was between deadlock through disagreement or agreement substantially on the French terms. There was very little 'give and take'; it was all 'take' and no 'give' as far as France was concerned.

The reason why the EEC survived the costly concessions made by five member Governments to France time after time was that the economic disadvantages of the concessions were mitigated by the almost uninterrupted creeping inflation and expansion that was proceeding within the EEC as everywhere else. Whether the Six were prosperous because of their association in the EEC or in spite of the cost they had to pay for the maintenance of that association, the fact remained that they were prosperous and could afford to pay France the high price she asked in return for remaining a member.

The real test will come when the sacrifices involved in maintaining a more or less united front will cease to be concealed by all-round prosperity. It remains to be seen how member nations will then react to concessions made at their expense during a period of economic depression, when they could ill afford to make such concessions, in conditions when concessions would not merely mean slower progress but an accentuation of setback. It makes quite a difference whether the arrangement operates against a background of fair weather or a background of bad weather.

Admittedly, there are historical instances in which a certain degree of economic integration prepared the way for political integration. The German *Zollverein* which paved the way to the Second German Empire of 1871–1918 was one of them. But it also shows that a mere customs union is also capable of leading to political union, so that from that point of view there seems to be no compelling reason for adopting such an advanced form of economic integration as the EEC is at the time of writing, let alone for adopting the much more advanced form that is envisaged.

Nor is it certain by any means that a much more advanced degree of economic integration would stand a better chance of ensuring the advent of political integration, or even a closer political alliance, than a mere customs union or even a free trade area in which each partner could retain its own external customs tariffs, on the lines of EFTA. There were of course disagreements also between the members of EFTA, but nothing that could be compared with the conflicts that arose from time to time within the EEC. And it can be stated without fear of contradiction that relationships between the nations belonging to EFTA are incomparably friendlier than those between nations belonging to the Common Market.

There are no such major conflicts of interest within EFTA as there are within the EEC, so that there is less reason for mutual resentment within the former than within the latter. The possibility that Britain or other EFTA countries might decide to join the EEC is loaded with controversy, and yet up to the time of writing it has failed to disturb the perfectly friendly relationship between the nine nations concerned. It is therefore arguable that a limited degree of economic integration is a more suitable first stage for political integration or for some lesser degree of political association than an advanced degree of economic integration which is bound to be pregnant with possibilities of sharp conflicts of basic interests.

Even the fundamental assumption that liberalisation of trade between countries necessarily makes for peace and goodwill between them cannot be accepted as axiomatic. There is at least one outstanding historical instance pointing to the opposite direction. Although the causes responsible for the French Revolution of 1789 had been manifold, the act that actually triggered it off and ensured its initial victory was the British–French trade treaty of 1787. It resulted in a heavy inflow of British textiles to France, leading to large-scale industrial unemployment. The desperate starving unemployed streamed to Paris. Having absolutely nothing to lose, the men dared to defy authority and formed the spearhead of the revolutionary movement that swept the *ancien régime* out of existence. The victory of the men whose violent action had been the result of an act liberating trade between two countries was followed by a war between those two countries, which lasted more than two decades.

My argument is also supported by the experience of the Austro-Hungarian monarchy before the First World War. One of the main reasons why the settlement of 1867 between the Habsburgs and Hungary failed to lead to friendly relationship between Austrians and Hungarians was that it had disregarded the Hungarian claim for the right to establish customs barriers against Austrian goods. It was felt in Hungary that, owing to the immense superiority of Austrian industries over Hungarian industries, the latter did not stand a fair chance against the competition of Austrian goods. This dissatisfaction had been largely responsible for the strong anti-Austrian feeling that prevailed in Hungary until it subsided in 1914 with the outbreak of the war. In that instance, as in the case of the British–French trade treaty of 1787, and in many other less well-known or less obvious instances, more freedom of trade between countries, so far from making for friendlier political relations between them, produced exactly the opposite effect.

It is of course possible to quote instances supporting the opposite thesis, showing that in given circumstances closer trade relationships did tend to create friendlier political relationships between countries. Far be it from me to try to argue that the less we are together, the happier (or the less unhappy) we must inevitably be. But the two instances quoted above suffice to cast doubt on the 'axiom' that liberalisation of trade relations necessarily makes for better political relations.

Last but by no means least, if liberalisation of trade is combined with other forms of economic integration, or even if it involves a uniform tariff for imports from outside the trading area, the chances are that relationships within the trading area are based on mutual distrust. The EEC set up a network of committees and elaborated an immense number of rules to stop the potential gaps in the application of its rules. These rules could fill a volume and their number is on the increase. Most of them mean interference with national economies, making things more complicated both for the Governments concerned and for business firms in the EEC countries. The friendly associates in the Common Market are watching each other with eagle eyes. Each Government is suspecting all the time the other five Governments or their nationals of attempts to circumvent the rules as far as possible. Such an atmosphere of mutual distrust does not tend to create an ideal relationship between participants in the EEC.

CHAPTER FOUR

The 'Big Market' Myth

IN the last two chapters I tried to prove that the popular argument in favour of joining the Common Market for the sake of paving the way for Western European political unity is utterly unconvincing and is unrealistic. This chapter and the following chapters examine whether it would be worth while for Britain to join the Common Market solely for the sake of economic considerations, in total disregard of political consequences. Before dealing with the disadvantages that are liable to arise from joining, we must examine the claims that joining the EEC would bring major economic advantages to Britain. Foremost among these claims is the argument that British industry would be bound to benefit by the enlargement of the area into which its goods are admitted free of duty in unlimited quantities.

That argument, which is all too familiar to students of elementary economics, is concerned, not with advanced economic integration such as is planned under the Treaty of Rome, but solely with the removal of customs barriers. But the establishment of a large market through the unification of separate markets creates more problems than it solves, and leaves a great many loopholes the stopping of which necessitates a wide variety of elaborate measures. In this chapter we are only concerned with the one aspect of economic integration with which economists from Adam Smith until the 'fifties were concerned – the creation of a large area in which goods produced in that area can be sold without any hindrance, irrespective of the part of the area in which they are produced.

The argument in favour of joining the Common Market is mainly based on the assumption that the widening of the area in which goods produced in the U.K. could be sold without the payment of duty on them would assist British industrial expansion considerably. There is no need to enlarge upon this aspect of the subject, which is very familiar ground. The larger the market the safer it is for industrial firms to increase their productive capacity and their output, thereby reducing the cost of production per unit of output.

Although this is basically true, it should not be regarded as representing the whole picture. Anyone who exaggerates this argument and is too dogmatic about it would be at a loss how to explain the high standard of living in small countries such as Switzerland and Sweden. Of course an explanation that is often made is that these countries were neutral during the two world wars and reaped the benefit of their neutrality, while most other advanced industrial countries suffered heavy losses. But even though this argument cannot be disregarded, its relative importance should not be exaggerated.

Given the existing industrial capacity of advanced nations, it does not take anything like a quarter of a century to make good the devastations and other losses suffered by belligerent countries. As far as the destruction of factories is concerned, and the dismantling of their equipment in Germany after her defeat, it proved to be an advantage in the long run. It enabled Germany to construct much more up-to-date industries than those of her victorious opponents whose industries had to patch up existing obsolete plants in many instances when it would have been to their advantage to scrap them and install the latest equipment. So war-time losses cannot be regarded as an unqualified disadvantage, and the fact that factories in Sweden and Switzerland remained intact during the war was not an unqualified advantage that could be held to account for the high standard of living in those countries.

Another small country, the Netherlands, can also boast of a high standard of living. It was high even before she became a member of the Common Market. This in spite of the war devastations she had suffered, the exploitation of her resources under Nazi occupation, and the confiscation of her immense investments in Indonesia. The standard of living rose in a spectacular way in another former belligerent country, Japan. Even though her population of over 100 million offers a more extensive market than that of Britain, it is not very much more extensive than that of EFTA and considerably more limited than that of the EEC, not to speak of the United States or of the Communist bloc. The 'Japanese miracle', together with the 'German miracle' and the 'Italian miracle' – both of which had preceded the establishment of the EEC – show that it is possible for hard-working nations to achieve progress and prosperity even if they do not possess markets of gigantic size.

The example of Sweden and of Switzerland in particular shows that it is possible to develop highly efficient industries in countries with a very limited domestic market. In many lines these countries are able to compete with rival industries which have the advantage of incomparably larger domestic markets. As for the Netherlands, her example shows that a small country is capable of creating gigantic firms, such as Royal Dutch, Unilever and Phillips, either independently or in partnership with foreign firms, which have extensive international ramifications and enjoy most of the advantages of their foreign rivals, notwithstanding the ability of the latter to depend on vastly superior domestic markets.

The size of the domestic market is undoubtedly an advantage, but it is by no means everything. What is infinitely more important is that the countries should be governed efficiently and that their populations should work hard. If only the size of the population counted, China and India would be the most prosperous countries instead of being among the least prosperous. If the people in a small country or in a medium-sized country such as Britain work hard, and if their hard work is well organised and encouraged by managements and public authorities, then such countries are bound to go from strength to strength in spite of the small size of their domestic market compared with that of much larger countries or combinations of countries. What matters infinitely more than the size of the market is the character of the people.

Advocates of joining the Common Market would like us to believe that the immense success of the United States, her achievement of the leading position among the nations in the economic and military sphere and her achievement of a unique standard of living and producing capacity, has been entirely, or almost entirely, the result of the large size of her domestic market. Beyond doubt, the existence of such a large market has helped. But in itself it would not have brought the United States to the position of the leading nation of the world had it not been for the character of the American people. Most of them are willing to work hard and have the utmost incentive to work hard. Being a relatively new country it is not tradition-ridden and welcomes and encourages every innovation in the technological sphere and in business organisation. American firms are willing to scrap equipment which is superseded by more recent inventions. Americans are essentially dynamic and they are given ample opportunity to benefit by their dynamism. In all probability the American nation would be almost as prosperous if the size of its market were a fraction of its present size, because where 10 million people or 5 million people work hard and efficiently, those 10 million people or 5 million people deserve to be prosperous and *are* prosperous.

Of course division of labour, which is one of the major conditions of efficiency, is facilitated by the large size of the market and by the large number of its inhabitants. On the law of averages the chances are that there are more scientists, inventors, first-class business brains, etc., in a nation of 200 million than in a nation of 20 million. But the fact that Switzerland has had more Nobel Prize winners per head of the population than any other country must remind us that numbers are not everything. The immense amount of money available in the United States for research and development does help a great deal. But Britain's post-war record in the sphere of inventions bears comparison with that of the United States, allowing for the much more limited resources at the disposal of her potential inventors.

Above all, big countries stand a better chance of creating giant firms than small or medium-sized countries. And we shall see in the next chapter that large firms undoubtedly have great advantages compared with smaller firms. But, as we saw above, a small country such as the Netherlands is also capable of bringing into existence giant firms the size of which is quite out of proportion to the size of the country where their head offices are situated. In any case, big business is becoming increasingly international. Giant firms are in a position to increase further by mergers across their national borders.

But even if we were to accept without reservation that the size of the domestic market is all-important, it would not prove the case for joining the Common Market. If the Commonwealth were to be amalgamated with EFTA it would create a free trade area with a potential absorbing capacity far in excess of that of the EEC. Admittedly the difference between wage levels in the EFTA countries and in the European-populated Commonwealth countries on the one hand and in the rest of the Commonwealth on the other hand might make it difficult for the former to admit unlimited quantities of industrial goods produced by the latter with the aid of cheap labour. But the problems arising from it would not be unsurmountable.

An even more ambitious and more promising extension of the trading area would be the creation of a North Atlantic Free Trade Area which would include the United States and Canada. That would provide far vaster markets without customs barriers between them than the EEC or even the amalgamation of the EEC with EFTA. By far the largest trading area could be created by the extension of NATO's scope to the economic field. Instead of aiming at economic integration of Western Europe for the sake of achieving political integration, the existing political alliance of countries which are allied to resist Communist-Imperialist aggression should be developed into a free trade area, or even a customs union. These possibilities are discussed in greater detail in Chapter 17. At present they are touched upon merely to remind ourselves that joining the EEC is by no means the only way of achieving membership in a large trading area.

In any case, the size of the trading area of the EEC is no

guarantee for British firms to be able to trade really freely in the countries that are included. The object of the Common Market is to enable firms in the member countries to trade in other member countries on an equal footing with firms in those countries. But in spite of the abolition of the customs barriers between them, it is the frequent experience of many firms that local firms in the countries to which they want to export are much 'more equal' than they are themselves. There are many other ways besides tariff walls for keeping out unwanted imports, and the abolition of the tariff walls between members of the EEC is in itself no guarantee for the free admission of each others' goods on an equal footing with locally produced goods.

The Brussels Commission set up a large number of committees in an effort to prevent the circumvention of the basic principle of the EEC by such methods as discriminatory transport charges, requirements regarding standards, licence requirements, etc. So long as there are possibilities of discrimination even in the absence of a tariff wall, the removal of the tariff wall is of limited use. That the establishment of a Common Market does not by itself create a large unrestricted trading area is indicated by the fact that trade within EFTA – which does not pretend to be a Common Market or even a customs union, merely a free trade area with separate customs tariffs against goods from third countries – expanded to a much higher degree than did trade within the EEC. It conveys the impression that the 'invisible tariff' within the EEC is more effective than it is within EFTA.

That 'invisible tariff' is reinforced by psychological influences. Even in the absence of tariff barriers, many people on the Continent prefer to buy national products. While the traditional free-trade mentality is deeply ingrained in the British people, with the exception of the Dutch people no continental nations have such traditions. It might take generations before the obstacle of economic nationalism disappears within the Common Market. Frenchmen prefer to buy French and Germans prefer to buy German even if goods from other EEC countries are slightly better or slightly cheaper. The difference has to be fairly marked before they overcome their preference for the respective national products. British exports would remain subject to that handicap even if Britain joined the Common Market.

Even customs officials in many countries deem it their patriotic duty to interpret customs regulations in a sense unfavourable to imports from abroad. They charge the higher tariff whenever they have a chance to do so. From this point of view admission into the Common Market would present a certain advantage, since there would be no duty to charge on goods imported from Britain. But since goods containing materials or components imported from outside the Common Market would remain subject to duty in proportion to such contents, the officials would still have an opportunity to do their patriotic duty according to their lights. And since a very high proportion of British goods has such import content, British exporters to the Common Market would be unduly optimistic to imagine that once we have joined the Common Market their troubles with customs authorities are finished and done with as far as their shipments to Common Market countries are concerned. The handicap of the uncertainty about the rates that would be charged would remain.

Moreover, continental customs officials are entitled to expect to be satisfied beyond any reasonable doubt that even goods containing ingredients of purely British origin are really 100 per cent British. Their scepticism in that respect, and overvaluation of the proportion of import contents in British goods, would give rise to frequent appeals against overcharging, causing prolonged uncertainty which even rulings on the appeals might not necessarily dispose of for good. Delays in receiving rebates of excess payments would have to be taken into consideration by continental importers, whether nationals of the countries concerned or affiliates of the British exporters.

Having regard to all this, it may well be asked whether the argument in favour of joining the Common Market for the sake of ensuring British goods access to continental markets free of duty is not overrated. Judging by the increase of British exports to the EEC, many British exporters are quite capable of overcoming the tariff wall. Possibly some lines of additional goods, which are at present unable to compete with goods produced within the EEC, would become competitive. On the other hand, EEC goods would become more competitive in Britain, and it is anyone's guess whether the benefits derived by British industry as a whole from the enlarged market, or the benefits derived by any individual British firms, would not be offset and more than offset by the increased competition in the home market.

In any case, apart altogether from the reductions and eventual elimination of tariff walls within the EEC and EFTA, the trend after the end of the war has been towards an all-round reduction of tariff walls, as a result of GATT, Kennedy Rounds, etc. Although at the time of writing there appears to be a possibility that this trend towards liberalisation of trade might become reversed, for the moment tariff walls outside the trading areas are not nearly as formidable as they were at one time.

Finally, customs unions and even the Common Market are liable to be affected by overvaluations and undervaluations of currencies, which are apt to constitute more effective barriers to competition than the remaining tariff walls. What is the use of removing the customs barriers on inter-EEC trade if EEC currencies are liable to become undervalued or overvalued? As I propose to show in Chapter 11, it would not materially help matters even if currencies within the EEC were kept rigidly stable in relation to each other, unless a single currency were issued under a single monetary authority which would ration currency and credit supplies to member countries. We are a very long way off that stage and I doubt whether it will ever be reached.

CHAPTER FIVE

Are Big Firms an Advantage?

WE saw in the last chapter that one of the advantages of large trading areas lies in the opportunity they provide for the expansion of individual firms into giant corporations. But judging by the example of the Netherlands, and owing to the growing internationalisation of big business, big countries do not possess the monopoly of producing giant firms. Nevertheless, statistics show that the large majority of the 'upper hundred' among the big firms are American. This does not necessarily mean that the only cause, or even the main cause, why so many American firms have grown so large is the size of their domestic markets. The existence of such markets does help considerably. But the dynamism of American businessmen, and the prolonged expanding basic trend in the United States rather than the actual size of the markets, was responsible for the growth of a great many individual firms and combines to their present gigantic size.

However, let us accept for the sake of argument that the expansion of the trading territory of the Common Market through the adhesion of Britain and other EFTA countries would greatly improve the chances of creating in Britain and in Western Europe business firms of a size comparable with that of their American rivals. The question we have to examine in this chapter is, would it be worth while for Britain to join the Common Market for the sake of the improved chances to expand British firms considerably?

Beyond doubt, an increase in the size of a firm or of a combine has considerable advantages and in given circumstances it is bound to strengthen the firm's competitive position against rival big firms in the United States or in other countries. In the first instance it is in a better position to increase its output and there-by to reduce costs of production per unit. Indeed the advantage of an enlarged market could not be exploited so satisfactorily unless the size of individual firms supplying the market is also expanded so as to be able to supply the additional goods at competitive prices. Given the prevailing high degree of employ-ment, an increase in the output without an increase in efficiency would necessarily mean an increase in the cost of production, because of competitive bidding by relatively small firms for the limited supply of manpower and because of an increase in the volume of production on which overtime pay is paid at higher rates. The additional demand for labour would shift the balance of power between employers and employees further in favour of the latter. The way to avoid this would be to achieve higher efficiency through amalgamations between firms which would eliminate overlapping. It would release manpower that would become available for increasing the output of the combined firm above the total output of the individual firms concerned.

What is perhaps even more important, large firms are in a position to spend more on research and development. Even if the amount allocated for that purpose by the combined firm is not larger than the total of the amounts allocated by the firms before their amalgamation, it would produce better results be-cause it would eliminate costly and time-wasting duplications. But the chances are that, thanks to its increased resources and to economies in other directions, the combined firm would be able to spend more on research and development than the total spent by the firms before their merger. It would be impossible to overestimate the importance of this. The pace of technological progress has been escalating considerably in recent years and is still escalating. The competitive capacity of rival firms depends on the extent to which they can keep up with this progress. Any firm which is unable to keep up with it because of lack of funds for research and development is liable to find itself at a grave and increasing disadvantage.

The money is needed not only for financing research and for applying inventions, innovations and improvements, but also for financing the replacement of the equipment rendered obsolete by new methods or by new requirements. This alone makes it essential for big firms, in order to prosper and even in order to survive, to become even bigger, with larger capital resources of their own and with larger borrowing facilities. Smaller firms might not be able to afford discarding comparatively new equipment long before its cost has been written off, and they would have to try to struggle on at a great disadvantage.

The question is, would Britain, by joining the EEC, improve her chances of producing super-firms? It would be easier for British firms and firms belonging to various EEC countries to amalgamate, especially if fiscal and legislative obstacles to such mergers were removed or mitigated. But there are already such amalgamated firms of long standing – Royal Dutch-Shell and Unilever, for instance – and the fact that Britain is outside the EEC does not constitute an unsurmountable obstacle to further mergers.

The authorities of the EEC appear to be in two minds about whether to encourage or discourage such mergers or even mergers between large firms in the same country. On the one hand, they are fully alive to the great advantages of possessing firms of a size comparable with that of their American opposite numbers. On the other hand, they are at least equally keen on avoiding anything that would restrain competition within the EEC, and they feel that if a firm achieves a quasi-monopolistic or oligopolistic position it produces just that effect. One of the major objectives of the Brussels Commission is to prevent or discourage any development that would deprive the Common Market of the full benefits of increased competition resulting from its creation.

Of course the Eurocrats or the Council of Ministers that has the final say could not possibly have it both ways. They would really prefer it if big firms were to confine themselves to co-ordinating their research programmes rather than amalgamate for the sake of pooling their research resources. But even though this is practicable to some extent, and it may be encouraged further, independent firms are naturally reluctant to share their secrets with their rivals, or to let them have the benefits derived from having a genius on their research staff. The EEC authorities will have to make up their minds sooner or later whether to prefer to have giant firms with less competition within the EEC but more competition outside the EEC, or with keener competition within the EEC but with less competition outside it. The EEC cannot get the best of both worlds. It might get the worst of both worlds if its authorities, being unable to make up their minds, should keep changing their attitude.

Of course there is ample room for two opinions about the extent of the advantages to be derived from growth beyond a certain limit, and also concerning the whereabouts of that limit. It is widely felt in many quarters that there is somewhere an optimum size beyond which further growth of the firm might cease to yield any advantages and might even entail disadvantages. Many experienced industrialists have reached the conclusion that it is to their interests to have several parallel factories rather than one super-factory. They deem it worth their while to increase initial expenditure by providing each factory with various separate facilities which could be provided at a much lower cost for a larger single factory with the same capacity as the total capacities of the separate factories.

But there are instances in which the claim that a certain firm has reached its optimum size savours distinctly of sour grapes. Some firms, having put forward that claim at one time of their development, embarked on another spell of growth subsequently when they came to be in a position to do so.

As far as Britain is concerned, growth beyond a certain limit was effectively prevented in many instances by rulings of the Monopolies Commission. But the policy pursued under British anti-monopoly legislation is not concerned with the optimum size of the firm. It is concerned with the proportion of its output to total requirements of the domestic market. Should adhesion to the Common Market increase demand for goods produced by firms which have been affected by the Government's anti-monopolist attitude, quite possibly that attitude might be relaxed.

If a substantial increase of our productivity through more expenditure on research and development depended on our decision whether to join the Common Market, the case for joining it would become much stronger. But it must be borne in mind that the limitations of the resources of British firms spent on research and development compared with those spent by American firms is not the only handicap under which British industry is working, not even the main handicap, aggravated as it is by heavy taxation that deprives it of resources for research and development.

It is the behaviour of British trade unions and their members that constitutes the main obstacle to technological progress in British industries. It even prevents the adequate application of inventions that are available, and it results in the maximum of disincentive for spending large amounts on research in quest of new inventions. What is the use of inventing labour-saving devices if their application would be handicapped by trade unions? The use of such devices is resisted by them to the utmost, and when trade unions eventually consent to their introduction it is on terms which make the change barely profitable. So long as this attitude continues to prevail, the increase in the amount of money available for research and development would not induce firms to make full use of the resources available. Why should they? They can hardly be blamed if they are not keen on spending merely to enable their workers to work even less against payment of even higher wages.

Moreover, there is in Britain strong trade union resistance to mergers, and such resistance would not abate if adhesion to the Common Market provided additional opportunities for mergers. Redundancy means costly strikes, to avoid which, or as a result of which, managements are forced to keep on their payroll the workers who would become superfluous either through amalgamations or through the application of labour-saving equipment. So long as the balance of power between managements and employees remains the same, British firms would not be able to take adequate advantage of any beneficial effect of higher expenditure on research and development through joining the

EEC. The costs of joining would not be offset by such benefits if the trade unions could help it.

Is there any reason to suppose that joining the Common Market would change the balance of power in favour of employers? This subject will be dealt with in the next chapter, which will examine the pro-Common Market argument that the efficiency of British industry would necessarily increase as a result of increased competition in the EEC.

CHAPTER SIX

Survival of the Fittest

As we saw in the last chapter, there is room for two opinions about the relative advantages and disadvantages of very large firms and about whether it would be worth while to join the EEC for the sake of the opportunity of increasing the size of big firms. But opinion in Britain is almost unanimously in favour of dogmatic belief in the advantages of more competition. The argument that by joining the EEC the extent of competition would increase does carry much weight. This, as the opinion in favour of the largest possible market, is part of the free-trader traditions of the British people. It is also one of the fundamental principles of the capitalist creed. One of the reasons why economic planning is on the whole unpopular in Britain lies in the belief that free competition with the minimum of Government interference is liable to produce much more favourable results than any avoidance of waste due to lack of planning or guidance. It seems probable that the majority of those who are in favour of joining the Common Market are influenced by the argument that in doing so competition would become distinctly keener.

The argument is valid beyond question in spheres in which the domestic economy depends for its supplies on a firm in a monopolistic or quasi-monopolistic position. The extent of its validity is decidedly less, however, in spheres in which the existing state of affairs is one of oligopoly – that is, when supplies depend on a small number of large firms. For the chances are that there is keener rivalry between a few competitors than between a large number of competitors. If there are only two or three fairly big shops of the same kind in a town, they are more likely to engage in cut-throat competition than if there were twenty or thirty smaller firms. It is often found that as a result of a series of amalgamations the firms which have survived become much keener competitors than they had been before.

It is therefore not justified to take it for granted that an increase in the number of firms in the same trading area as a result of the extension of that trading area would necessarily lead to keener competition. Nor is the argument that is encountered at times, that competition with firms in other countries is liable to be keener than with firms in our own country, very convincing. It is true that businessmen in the same town, who know each other personally, belong to the same clubs and meet each other socially might be more inclined to hold their punches when competing with each other than they are when competing with strangers. But while that may be so in respect of rivals in the same town or in the same district, there is no reason why there should be a different spirit of competitiveness between a London firm and a Düsseldorf firm than between a London firm and a Manchester firm.

It is of course possible that rivals abroad may be more efficient in some lines, or that circumstances are more in their favour, in which case they stand a chance of competing their British rivals out of existence once the tariff barriers between their goods are removed. Confronted with foreign rivals which are more efficient or are favoured by local advantages, British firms might be spurred to an extra effort in order not to be competed out of existence. If successful they would survive thanks to their increased efficiency. Otherwise they would have to go out of business or witness a decline in their turnover. The removal of customs barriers between the U.K. and the EEC would produce many such victims in all countries concerned.

This is the 'survival of the fittest' argument in favour of joining the Common Market. Let only the most efficient firms, working under the most favourable conditions, survive in every country. The net result of the disappearance of the less efficient, and of firms which, however efficient they may be, would be up against the more favourable local conditions amidst which their foreign rivals operate, would be, it is claimed, the best utilisation of the productive resources of all countries for the benefit of all. Let everything be produced where it can be produced under the most advantageous conditions. That is the basic aim of free trade.

This philosophy disregards the human element. Dogmatic free traders are indifferent to the widespread losses that the application of the system inflicts on a large number of business firms which go bankrupt and on a much larger number of their employees who lose their jobs. Progress can seldom be achieved without making sacrifices and it does not hurt as much if the victims are other people. They are expected to pay the price of the increased efficiency that would result from the introduction of new elements into competition through joining the EEC. It is argued that the initial cost would be more than made good – if not to the individuals concerned then to the entire community – by gains in other directions, and by the general long-run advantages of making the most efficient use of productive resources. Each country would have victims of the change, but on balance they stand to benefit, if not immediately at any rate in the long run.

But only experience would show in which countries would gains outweigh losses resulting from the change. Britain would certainly be exposed to painful losses as a result of joining the Common Market, very often through no fault of the British firms but owing to the more favourable conditions in which foreign rivals are able to produce goods competing with British goods in the home market. It is anybody's guess whether or not our gains would outnumber and outweigh our losses. Even if they did, it would be small comfort for the shareholders whose life's savings would be wiped out as a result of the drastic change in the system to know that other firms have grown more prosperous as a result of the same change.

Even if the losses suffered by the victims among business firms and their shareholders were disregarded, it would be more difficult to disregard the resulting loss of employment by a large number of employees in industries hit by the change.

It is true, in theory it would merely mean a reallocation of labour, for the firms which benefit by the change would absorb the former manpower of firms which came to be competed out of business. But amidst conditions prevailing in Britain the reallocation of labour would be no easy matter. At best it would inflict considerable losses and major inconvenience to have to change residence and/or to have to be retrained for a new occupation. At worst it would mean prolonged if not permanent unemployment for those who would lose their jobs. In existing circumstances a large part of such unemployment would be voluntary, because unemployment relief in various forms is granted on such a generous scale that many employees who lost their jobs would prefer to remain unemployed until they are given jobs in the same district and in the same occupation.

It is therefore optimistic oversimplification to assume that the manpower of firms victimised by the change would be simply transferred to firms that would gain by the change. The latter would find it very difficult to increase their manpower in order to cope with the increased volume of orders received from EEC countries. Such expanding industries would be short of manpower in spite of the increased unemployment in other industries or in other districts. To meet their requirements they would have to bid for the limited number of hands available, and their competitive bidding for labour would further strengthen the bargaining position of the trade unions and their members. Wage inflation would become accentuated.

If, as is probable, reallocation of labour should prove to be more difficult in Britain than in other countries of the EEC, the firms which initially gained by her entry into the Common Market would soon lose their competitive advantage, and might even find themselves at a disadvantage, as a result of the escalation of the wage inflation in their industries in particular and in Britain in general. Should this situation arise, British industry would lose both on the swings and on the roundabouts. This is indeed what is likely to happen as a result of the stepping-up of competition through joining the EEC. Although the 'English disease' has spread over Western Europe, it is still more virulent in its country of origin than in Germany or in other industrial countries. In none of the EEC countries is the balance of power so strongly in favour of the trade unions as in Britain, and in none of them are the trade unions so helpless in face of unofficial industrial action. For this reason, in none of the countries is the benefit derived from Britain's entry by competitive firms likely to be so short-lived as in Britain.

Admittedly, British industry might benefit in a general way by the shake-up caused as a result of joining the Common Market. The appearance of new competitors abroad might increase competition even between British firms. It is also possible on the other hand that, in face of the new rivals, British firms might join forces by concluding market-sharing arrangements. Such arrangements are known to have been concluded in the past across borders also.

There is no reason to take it for granted that the Common Market necessarily leads to the survival of the fittest. There can be a wide variety of ways in which the continued existence of the less fit is ensured in the Common Market. The Governments concerned might circumvent the letter and spirit of the Common Market rules and subsidise or protect their firms in some form so as to safeguard them against being competed out of existence by more efficient firms in other Common Market countries. They might even assist their nationals sufficiently to enable them to compete more efficient firms abroad out of existence, or at any rate to gain ground at their expense. Admittedly, the Brussels Commission and its various committees are making a supreme effort to stop these loopholes. But it remains to be seen to what extent their exertions will prove really effective.

Moreover, it would not be of any use for a British firm to be more efficient than a firm in a Common Market country if sterling is overvalued compared with the currency of that country. Admittedly, its chances of overcoming the handicap imposed by an overvalued sterling on British trade would improve as a result of the removal of the customs barrier for its exports to the country concerned. But sterling is liable to become even more overvalued after Britain has joined the Common Market as a result of joining it. The gain derived from the removal of the customs barrier might not then enable British exporters to compete successfully against less efficient firms in the Common Market. Fiscal and other differences are also liable to protect the less efficient firm on the Continent from British competition in spite of the removal of customs barriers.

It must also be borne in mind that British economic activity that is liable to be affected by any increased competition as a result of our entry into the EEC represents only part of the British economy. Sheltered industries, especially service industries, which represent a large and increasing proportion of our economy, are of course immune to foreign competition and would remain immune.

In any case, practical experience does not always support the argument about the all-curing effect of a high degree of competition. No industries in the U.K. are exposed, or could be exposed in any conceivable circumstances, to foreign competition more than the shipbuilding and ship-repairing industries. And yet for a great many years they remained among the least efficient industries of the country. Even their modernisation and the increase of their efficiency through amalgamations would not have saved many shipyards from the consequences of the 'English disease' if it had not been for the shipping boom which ensured ample orders to all shipyards capable of building or repairing them.

CHAPTER SEVEN

Exploiting Growth-Hysteria

ONE of the most tempting inducements held out by those in favour of joining the Common Market is that it would step up Britain's highly inadequate growth, thereby raising the standard of living. Of course we are all in favour of a higher rate of growth and a higher standard of living, just as we are in favour of fair weather, good health and everlasting happiness for all. A thousand pities that they cannot be brought about by merely wishing them to come about.

If the British public could be persuaded that by joining the Common Market Britain's national income would rise faster, and more goods and services would become available for all, support for joining the Common Market would increase enormously. Under the influence of the prevailing growth-hysteria people are willing to put up even with accelerating inflation for the sake of stepping up the rate of growth. They would be only too willing to put up with many disadvantages that would arise from joining the Common Market if they were made to believe that at that price their standard of living would increase faster. But to the extent to which support for joining the Common Market would be obtained through that tempting promise it would be obtained very largely under false pretences.

Of course it is easy to produce figures in support of any argument. Gullible people may be impressed by statistical 'evidence' produced for their benefit to show that national income and real wages in the EEC have been rising at a higher rate than in Britain. But the conclusions derived from such selective presentation of statistics can be discredited by the fact that the rate of growth in some Common Market countries was faster *before* they became members of the EEC than after the gradual application of the Treaty of Rome; and that in a number of countries outside the EEC the rate of growth was higher than that of any country in the EEC. The size of the market is by no means the only factor to determine the rate of growth.

It is of course arguable that, had it not been for the Common Market, the rate of growth in Germany and Italy would have fallen even more after the completion of the 'German miracle' and the 'Italian miracle'. Such contentions can never be proved or disproved. Nor for that matter can the contention be proved that British capital investment, output and real wages would have risen at a faster rate if Britain had joined the Common Market from the very start, or that their rise would be accelerated if she joined it now. Figures can support any thesis, according to the way in which they are marshalled. And many people simply want to believe in them.

What is clearly evident is that, whether in or out of the Common Market, Britain would have been handicapped by the demoralisation of the British working classes during the 'sixties. Dealing with this subject in detail in my *Decline and Fall? Britain's Crisis in the Sixties*, I sought to draw attention to the sharp contrast between the behaviour of trade unions and their members in Britain and their behaviour in other industrial countries. I described the symptoms of the 'English disease', manifesting itself mainly in excessive wage demands unaccompanied by higher productivity, in the frequency of strikes, many of them for trifling reasons, in overtime bans, go-slows, malingering, in the general malevolent attitude of employees towards their employers and their utter indifference towards the interests of the community and even of their fellow-workers.

All this could not easily be proved by statistics, especially as much of the official statistical material is deficient or even misleading. An outstanding example was provided by the figures of the number of days lost through strikes every month published by the Department of Employment and Productivity.

These figures were used for years by politicians and trade unionists to prove that Britain's troubles were *not* due to loss of output through strikes, seeing that the number of days lost through strikes was lower than in many other industrial countries. The British figures claimed to cover also the number of days lost through workers having to be laid off through strikes by other workers. But a careful reading of all explanatory notes that accompany the statistical tables once a year discloses the fact that only workers laid off *in the same factory* are taken into account. Even workers laid off by the same firm in other plants are excluded, and of course so are workers laid off by other firms and in other industries. So while the official figures were *technically* true (albeit only just so), they were deliberately misleading because they sought to convey the impression that they were comprehensive. They misled even some economists who ought to have known better. They enabled propagandists to whitewash trade unions and unofficial strikers and shield them from well-earned condemnation by public opinion.

Anyhow, there are no figures available, not even deliberately misleading figures, about the losses of output through go-slows and other industrial action or inaction. It is the spirit of the so-called working classes that is so obviously different from that of their opposite numbers in Germany, Italy, Japan and other countries where workers do *not* aim at giving as little as possible in return for their pay.

It is because such a spirit does *not* prevail on the Continent – or at any rate it did not prevail until recently – that the Common Market countries are doing better than Britain. So are, for that matter, Britain's partners in EFTA. Even France, where the bad behaviour of workers in 1968 greatly surpassed, for a short time, anything experienced in Britain throughout the 'sixties, staged a remarkably speedy recovery. Conceivably this was because the Communist trade unions received instructions from Moscow to abstain from sabotaging the efforts of a Government which pursued a foreign policy that suited the Soviet Government's interests.

A familiar argument is that Britain's slow growth was due to the inadequacy of capital investment by her industries. Even if this were true, the inadequacy of investment is attributable to the fact that too high a proportion of the output is consumed – you cannot eat your cake and invest it – and that, as was pointed out earlier, trade unions in Britain resist modernisation and discourage managements from becoming more efficient by means of amalgamations or by installing costly labour-saving equipment.

The question is, would it make any difference to the attitude of trade unions and their members if Britain joined the EEC? It is repeated to boredom that, under the effect of keener foreign competition, managements would make a supreme effort to become more efficient. But resistance to redundancy would become, if anything, even stronger when many workers of firms affected by increased competition become unemployed. It is true, if the British system of taxation were to be remodelled in accordance with the Western European system, so that direct taxation were replaced by value-added tax, more money would become available to be ploughed back into industry. But trade unions would continue to prevent effectively the modernisation of plants since it would mean reallocation of labour involving some degree of additional temporary unemployment.

Even if in spite of all handicaps and discouragements British industries that would stand to benefit by free access to the Common Market were to succeed in modernising their plants, it would not necessarily mean that they could benefit by investing additional capital. Recent experience of the British shipbuilding industry seems to indicate that, so long as the workers' behaviour does not change, no amount of modernisation could benefit Britain. More than one of our shipyards, which are considered to be among the most efficient in the whole world, was brought to the verge of bankruptcy. Frequent strikes and other trade union practices prevented them from completing the ships for the date of the contract. And owing to the sharp rise in wages during the long period between the signing of the contract and the completion of the ships, wage increases resulted in a dead loss.

As we saw in Chapter 6, it would be useless to expect miracles from the increased competition that would result from joining the Common Market. A relatively moderate increase in unemployment caused by that additional competition would not give the much-needed shock that might bring the British worker to his senses. It is only if increased competition and the resulting unemployment should assume such high proportions as to make the worker realise that his job is endangered unless he puts in an honest day's work for his high pay that the much-needed change might occur. But then such a change would come about through any crisis or major depression regardless of the cause. It is pointless to agitate in favour of joining the Common Market merely for the sake of creating a sufficient degree of unemployment to reduce the bargaining position of the trade unions and make workers realise that they have to work in order to keep their jobs.

Moreover, whatever other effect such a drastic remedy would produce, it would most certainly not increase the rate of growth. Indeed it would actually cause a major setback. Nor would it cause an increase in real wages – unless and until the British worker, whose standing grievance is that his money wages are lower than those of workers in the EEC, comes to work as hard as his continental fellow-worker. At present, allowing for the difference in productivity, he is paid much higher wages than the hard-working German or Italian worker, or even the French worker.

It remains of course to be seen whether the new Conservative Government's various policies will result in changes calling for a revision of the conclusions reached in this chapter as indeed in other chapters. At the time of writing it would be premature to make any forecasts. But if the new Government were to succeed where its Socialist predecessor and even the previous Conservative Government failed, then Britain would be certain to prosper and her rate of growth would increase, whether or not she joined the Common Market.

CHAPTER EIGHT

The Balance Must Balance

HAVING had endless trouble with balance of payment deficits ever since the war, it is no wonder that the British public is ready and eager to listen to any proposals which are claimed to provide a solution of that problem. I have often wondered what proportion of those in Britain who are in favour of joining the Common Market are in favour of it because they have been persuaded, or have succeeded in persuading themselves, that once we are inside the EEC our balance of payments worries would become a matter of the past. British industries would have at their disposal a large area in which, they assume, it would be as easy to sell as in the domestic markets. Although the EEC, even in its enlarged form, is not expected to be self-supporting, its member countries (including Britain) would depend on their exports to countries outside their common customs territory to a much smaller degree.

Within the EEC there are of course expected to be surpluses and deficits on the trade between member countries. But according to advocates of the Common Market this would not give rise to any crises such as we experienced on many occasions during the last quarter of a century. It is one of the favourite myths that in the absence of customs barriers trade between countries would tend to balance automatically, owing to the effect of one-sided trading on supply–demand relationship within each country. If prices in one of the countries within the EEC rise more than in other countries, the resulting increase of imports and decline of exports tends to increase the supply of goods, while at the same time the effect on domestic production and employment tends to reduce demand for goods. According to dogmatic free traders it is only the existence of customs barriers and other forms of restriction on the international movement of goods that prevents the automatic self-correcting operation of export surpluses or import surpluses.

Moreover, the automatic operation of the system within the Common Market is supplemented, or will be supplemented once economic integration is completed, by co-operation between the Governments concerned. Any one-sided trend will be investigated and means will be devised for offsetting it as far as possible. If a currency is obviously out of equilibrium the Government concerned is authorised to devalue or revalue it. This is supposed to be the function of the IMF, but it is claimed that such adjustments could be effected much more simply within the EEC. This aspect of the subject will be dealt with in greater detail in the next chapter; here let it be sufficient to point out that France devalued and Germany revalued in 1969 without authorisation by the EEC authorities, indeed without even consulting them. There is nothing in the EEC as it is organised at present to facilitate the process of balancing foreign trade by parity adjustment that could not be effected by entirely independent countries, with or without authorisation by the IMF.

Up to the time of writing there has been very little evidence of any other form of intervention within the EEC to correct trade balances by actively assisting the deficit countries to export more or import less. As for surplus countries, the remedy lies in their own hands. But so far they have shown little inclination to take more effective steps to reduce their surpluses in relation to fellow-members of the EEC than they showed in respect of their surpluses in relation to the rest of the world. In any case, excessive Government interference with trade would be contrary to the spirit of free trade within the EEC.

The theoretical assumption is that once trade barriers are removed, any disequilibrium tends to correct itself in the absence of artificial measures. Whether this survival of nineteenth-century liberalism will survive under the strain of persistently one-sided trading between partners in the EEC remains to be seen. Of course if and when economic and political integration should ever achieve its goal, import surpluses or export surpluses between member countries of the EEC would matter as little as import surpluses or export surpluses between two English counties, or at any rate between two States of the United States. But that goal is nowhere within sight and even the most optimistic prophets would hardly dare to forecast its materialisation for a great many years.

In the meantime, however, the balance of payments between countries of the EEC could be balanced by means of reciprocal financial assistance, and even more by the simple device of laying down the rule that the surplus countries should accept the IOUs of the deficit countries and hold them pending the turn of the tide of trade. Something along such lines was already actually in operation for a number of years even before the existence of the EEC, in the 'fifties when the European Monetary Union acted as a clearing-house for inter-European claims and liabilities. In doing so it accumulated currencies of deficit countries which the latter were expected to redeem in the course of time. In this respect up to the time of writing the EEC has not yet reached the stage already reached before its existence. But there are possibilities for progress in that direction.

The fashionable theory is that it should be the responsibility of surplus countries to enable their debtors to pay their debts. That theory may perhaps stand a better chance of being put into operation within the EEC than all over the world or even all over the free world on this side of the Iron Curtain. But I am convinced that the application of the principle would not produce too satisfactory results. It would be too tempting for idle nations and for irresponsible Governments to take undue advantage of the willingness of surplus countries, or for some central organisation acting as a clearing-house for surpluses and deficits, to allow them to become perennial deficit countries.

That system, which would be ideal if its use were confined to tiding over temporary difficulties, is certain to be misused by some countries. It would most certainly be misused by Britain if by the time of her admission into the EEC it should be in operation, unless she recovered by then from the 'English disease' and acquired sufficient determination not to relapse into it, having regard to the maximum of temptation coupled with the maximum of opportunity provided by the willingness of the surplus countries of the EEC to accept her IOUs.

Indeed, it was quite conceivably the prospects of obtaining such assistance from the EEC after the generosity of the United States or her capacity to assist us had been exhausted that must have induced Mr Wilson to change his mind between March and September 1966 about joining the Common Market. He must have envisaged the advent of the dread moment when the United States would no longer be able or willing to underwrite Britain's apparently perennial trade deficit. So he may have felt impelled to try to reinsure his Government against that contingency by preparing the way for the possibilities of drawing on the increasing resources of Western Europe.

Mr Wilson and other 'converts' in favour of joining may have felt that, once we are inside the Common Market, it would cease to matter whether our accounts with the rest of the EEC were balanced. It would become their responsibility to enable us somehow to pay our debts arising from their surpluses on their trade with us, as an alternative to allowing us to owe those debts in perpetuity. In other words, it came to be assumed that the EEC would owe Britain a living and that it would be for Britain to determine how good that living should be.

But such an arrangement would be as if one's bank manager granted one unlimited overdraft facilities on the 'repay as you please' principle. Those who think on such lines – whether in connection with our situation within the Common Market or in connection with the allocation of Special Drawing Rights or under a system of floating exchanges, in connection with our situation in the world at large – optimistically assume that the sky would be the limit to the willingness of surplus countries to allow their surpluses to be owed. They are well advised to re-

read in La Fontaine's immortal poem *La Cigale et la Fourmi* about the answer given by the provident ant to her neighbour the irresponsible grasshopper when the latter applied to her for winter assistance.

According to one of the first lessons in the study of foreign exchange – a lesson which, however elementary, is often overlooked – the balance of payments must always balance just as the two sides of a balance sheet must always equate. The question is how the balance is achieved. If it is achieved through running up external liabilities – which constitute a capital item in the balance of payments – there is no cause to be pleased about the balance being 'balanced'. If it is too easy to balance a deficit on current foreign trade by borrowing abroad or by simply owing the amount due for import surpluses, there is no inducement for Governments or for nations to aim at surpluses, or at least at equilibrium, instead of having perennial deficits.

If we joined the Common Market and if the other member countries made it too easy for Britain to remain in the red, it would mean that the British worker could work even less for even higher unearned wages, and the British Government could overspend with impunity to an even higher degree. There would be no incentive for resisting the wage plunder and the waste of public moneys. Why should we not all have a grand time instead, since our deficits would be looked after by Governments and countries which are foolish enough to practise self-restraint? Encouragement of such an attitude by a willingness of the other EEC countries to put up with it, at any rate for some time, would remove one of the few remaining obstacles to an escalated debasement of the British character as well as to an escalated debasement of sterling.

Of course sooner or later the surplus countries of the EEC would have to call a halt. But by that time Britain's unpaid external liabilities would have become gigantic and her capacity to repay would have declined considerably under the demoralising influence of the ease with which it had been possible to live on overdrafts.

Hitherto we have been discussing balance of payments problems within the EEC. Our next task is to examine the position in respect of Britain's trade with countries outside the EEC, in conjunction with the broader problem of the EEC's balance of payments in relation to the rest of the world. Even though the EEC aims at replacing trade with the outside world as far as possible by trade within the Common Market, it does not and could not possibly achieve self-sufficiency. As constituted at present, it has associated countries, mainly outside Europe, and they provide various goods which are not produced and could not be produced within the EEC countries. There are, moreover, various goods which cost much less if they are produced outside the EEC. Provided that they do not compete with agricultural products of the EEC, and provided that they are able to overcome the external tariff barrier, their import is not resisted. As already mentioned, the post-war trend has been towards freer international trade, stimulated by GATT, Kennedy Rounds and other reciprocal concessions. The Common Market has not kept aloof from this trend.

Like the trade of any country or group of countries, the trade of the EEC with the rest of the world is certain to have its ups and downs. If, as seems conceivable at the time of writing, the stability of EEC currencies should be maintained more rigidly than that of other currencies, the EEC countries as a whole might easily find themselves handicapped in their exports by the effects of devaluations by other countries. In that case the EEC as a whole is likely to have an adverse balance in relation to outside countries. Should the deficit assume considerable size and should it continue over a period of years, it would deplete the reserves of the EEC countries and increase their external indebtedness – including drawings from the IMF. On the other hand, if non-EEC currencies were kept stable while the domestic price levels of the countries concerned rose to a larger degree than the price levels in EEC countries, then the external position of the EEC as a whole would strengthen further.

It is of course impossible to make any forecasts about the

relative degree of inflation within and outside the EEC. On the one hand the Governments and the public in most EEC countries are inclined to favour hard money. On the other hand, should progress towards integration be accompanied by an increase in reciprocal economic assistance, it might encourage at least some of the countries to adopt a less sound attitude towards inflationary pressure. All this is of course bound to be in the realm of conjecture.

What is essential is to realise that the balance of payments of the EEC as a whole is of little consequence from the point of view of individual members unless and until the EEC adopts a single unified currency. This subject will be discussed in the next chapter. Until such a major change takes place, the balances of payment and the currencies that matter are those of individual EEC countries.

The question is, how is the British balance of payments in relation to countries outside the EEC likely to be affected if Britain joined the EEC? As we saw earlier in this chapter, the prospects of easy assistance from her EEC partners are liable to aggravate the 'English disease'. Should my pessimism to that effect prove to be correct, it would of course affect the British balance of payments not only within the EEC but also in relation to countries outside the EEC. Possibly assistance within the EEC would assume the form of surplus EEC countries financing readily their surpluses in relation to Britain. To that extent there would be more inducement to import in excess of exports from EEC countries than from countries outside the EEC. Conceivably the difference might be sufficient to ensure that Britain would balance her trade with the outside world by replacing import surpluses from non-EEC countries with import surpluses from EEC countries.

On the other hand the possibility of an all-round deterioration resulting from the demoralising effects of free and easy assistance within the EEC must be envisaged. In addition to incurring debts within the family, Britain might be strongly tempted to incur debts also outside the family. For if the Government should find it too easy, thanks to having joined the Common Market, to allow the balance of payments to deteriorate, it might become reluctant to resist inflation. Yet owing to the initial costs of joining the EEC, and also to its subsequent current costs – about which more will be said in Chapter 12 and in subsequent chapters – Britain would have to produce a substantial export surplus if she wants to avoid increasing her external debts as the only possible means to pay for the costs of joining the Common Market.

From that point of view, indeed from any point of view, it would not make any difference whether Britain's surplus or deficit were on her account with EEC countries or on her account with non-EEC countries. But the chances are that diversion of her purchases from other continents to Western Europe would react on her exports to the other continents. The abandonment of Commonwealth Preference alone and the application of an external tariff on non-EEC imports would cause the countries affected to curtail their purchases from Britain. In any case, the extension of the EEC over Britain and possibly over a number of other European countries is liable to affect the prosperity of other continents and therefore their capacity to buy British goods. This would mean that, in the absence of a very marked expansion of world trade, the effect of joining the Common Market would be a decline not only in Britain's relative share in non-EEC trade but also in the absolute quantities of her trade with non-EEC countries.

Whatever trade with the EEC Britain would gain as a result of joining the EEC she would be liable to lose in relation to countries outside the EEC. Yet it is a popular assumption that any gain of trade with the EEC resulting from joining the EEC would be a *net* addition to our existing trade. Even if Britain had the spare productive capacity to add materially to her total exports in addition to meeting domestic demand, by joining the EEC she would merely divert her exports as well as her imports from her other trading partners. To the extent to which British industries are working to capacity this is of course quite obvious. But even to the extent to which some industries have unused capacity the same result is liable to arise, owing to the 'English disease', which prevents many British firms from working to capacity without exposing themselves to excessive wage demands.

The cessation of Commonwealth Preference would enable rival industrial countries to capture British markets in the Commonwealth. The decline of British imports from the Commonwealth and from other countries outside the EEC is liable to produce a psychological effect on importers in those countries, even in the absence of official measures of retaliation.

The common external tariff of the EEC, if adopted by Britain, would reduce industrial protection against imports from non-EEC countries, according to the Confederation of British Industries, by about $2\frac{1}{4}$ per cent on the average. This, in addition to the complete disappearance of protection against goods from the EEC, might make an appreciable difference to the volume of manufactured imports. As already pointed out, there will be less incentive for countries outside the EEC to buy British if we restricted their exports to Britain, apart altogether from the possibility that their capacity to import would also suffer through a diversion of our purchases of their goods.

All this is of course necessarily very vague. The truth of the matter is that there is absolutely no possibility of making any reliable estimates about the effect of our joining the Common Market on our trade either with the EEC or with the rest of the world. Any effort to quantify the possible effect is sheer conjecture and should not pretend to be anything else. There are far too many unknown and uncertain factors to make it possible to put forward any dependable forecasts concerning the balance of payments even in the absence of such a basic change as adhesion to the EEC would undoubtedly be. I always envy the cocksureness of the National Institute of Economic and Social Research and other bodies which boldly forecast the trade figures for the next quarter or two, undeterred by the large number of occasions on which their forecasts proved hopelessly off the mark. Even to the extent to which the balance of payments depends on Government policies, the Government concerned is unable to foresee what changes of policies it will feel impelled to make under the effect of changes in the situation or prospects, or under political pressure. Still less are we able to foresee what policies a hundred or more other Governments will pursue. Least of all are we in a position to predict how the large number of firms and individuals on whom the volume of our exports and imports ultimately depends will behave. If ever any balance of payments forecast happens to come near to being correct, it is through sheer accident.

All we can say with a high degree of assurance is that it would be idle to expect a miraculous lasting improvement in the British balance of payments as a result of joining the Common Market, and the chances are that in the short run at any rate our balance of payments would deteriorate considerably. One of the main reasons for this, if not *the* main reason, is that it would be unduly optimistic to expect that the change would cure the 'English disease' at home. And there is no reason for supposing that it would spread the 'English disease' abroad to our benefit to any larger degree than it is already spread. This aspect of the subject is discussed in the next chapter.

CHAPTER NINE

Will 'English Disease' Spread or Be Cured?

WE saw in Chapter 7 that the only hope for accelerated growth for Britain, whether within or outside the Common Market, would be her recovery from the 'English disease'. We also saw in Chapter 8 that the prospects of Britain's balance of payments depend on the relative extent to which the 'English disease' will develop in Britain and in the Common Market. While growth in Britain would not accelerate through the spreading of the 'English disease' abroad, her balance of payments might improve as a result of the spreading of the 'English disease' in other countries.

At the time of writing, the balance of payments argument does not figure so prominently in Britain as it did in the late 'sixties, for the perennial deficit was replaced in 1969–70 by a substantial surplus. But the claim put forward by Socialists that this was a 'British miracle' comparable with the German, Italian, Japanese and other 'miracles' of the earlier post-war years is entirely unfounded.

The British worker did not work any harder in 1969–70 than in previous years. Quite on the contrary, there was a sharp increase in the number of strikes and in the extent of other labour troubles. The increase in national production slowed down to such an extent that growth came almost to a standstill. The extent of indiscipline in industry and elsewhere increased. Government expenditure and municipal spending continued to increase, even though the rate of increase slowed down. It is true, the Budget was not only balanced but produced a substantial revenue surplus. But this was not done by cutting down expenditure. It was done by adding to the heavy burden of taxation. The extent of wage demands and of wage concessions increased at least fivefold within a brief space of twelve months.

If in spite of all this the British balance of payments improved in 1969–70 this was largely the result of a deterioration in labour conditions in the United States and in other industrial countries. Workers in those countries seem to have caught the 'English disease'. The number of strikes increased everywhere and trade unions on the Continent, in the United States and even in Japan came to follow the British example by putting forward and enforcing grossly excessive wage claims under the pressure of the increasing number of unofficial strikes. Thanks to this, Britain's relative position improved as a result of the deterioration of conditions elsewhere.

Does this necessarily mean that, should Britain join the Common Market, the relative competitive position of British industries would now bear comparison with that of industries in other countries in the Common Market? Would the removal of customs barriers between Britain and the EEC benefit British industries at least to the same extent as it would benefit the industries of Western Europe? It depends almost entirely on the relative extent to which the EEC countries have caught, and would be likely to catch, the 'English disease' and on the relative extent to which the 'English disease' would become aggravated or would abate in its country of origin.

As far as Germany is concerned, in spite of the recent escalation of wage demands and increase in the number of strikes, there was no sign of the high degree of indiscipline experienced in British industries. The number of wildcat strikes increased but was still incomparably smaller, and German workers did not allow themselves to be influenced by political troublemakers to anything like the same extent as British workers. The speed with which France recovered by 1970 from the chaos of 1968–69 indicated that the extent of the demoralisation of the French workers was more moderate than that of the British workers. Or possibly the explanation lies in the pro-Soviet orientation of French foreign policy referred to earlier, and in France's detachment from

NATO, which may have induced the Soviet Government to instruct the powerful French Communist Party to pull its punches. The Italian worker, like the German worker and unlike the British worker since the war, is fundamentally hard-working, so that the Italian economy survived the spate of trouble that it experienced in 1964–65 and in 1968–69, threatening on more than one occasion the stability of the country. As for the Japanese situation, productivity kept pace to a large extent with the sharp rise in wages enforced by a series of unprecedented strikes.

At the time of writing it looks as if the advantage gained by British industry from troubles abroad would prove to be short-lived – this in spite of the change of Government which made it possible to make a genuine effort to restore some degree of discipline in industry. But on the whole it seems probable that the relative degree of the 'English disease' will change once more to Britain's disadvantage, if it has not done so already.

The question is, how would Britain's entry into the Common Market affect the situation and the prospects in this respect? This is by far the most important question concerning the effect of joining the EEC on Britain's balance of payments and on other aspects of the British economy.

The White Paper on the costs of joining the EEC candidly admitted that a wide range of estimates of that effect is possible. The net balance of the guesstimates of the relevant items depends on the degree of optimism or pessimism of those who make the guesstimate. And there are two all-important spheres in respect of which it is not possible even to make a guesstimate. In the crucial area of our financial contribution to the Community Agricultural Fund, 'there is just not a sufficient basis, in advance of the negotiations, for making reliable assumptions either about its costs or our share in it'. And even if an agreement is reached about the rules, it is just not possible to make reliable estimates about how it would work out in practice.

Nor could all the official and unofficial publications containing an impressive number of statistics based on actual results or on estimates of future results provide any guidance as to what we are to expect about the way in which and the extent to which Britain's entry into the Common Market is likely to affect the 'English disease' in Britain and in other Common Market countries.

As pointed out in Chapter 6, those who have a quasi-religious belief in the all-curing effect of competition are convinced that under the influence of the influx of goods from the EEC countries where most workers are still in the habit of doing a full day's work for their pay, British workers would adopt willy-nilly that habit for fear of being competed out of their jobs. There is no justification whatsoever for such optimism. The British motor industry enjoys a high degree of protection, but it does not prevent the import of a large and increasing number of foreign cars which are competitive in the British market in spite of the customs barrier. Once the customs barrier is removed, the number of foreign cars imported is certain to increase considerably. But it is not likely to reduce the 'English disease' in the motor industry.

Is there any reason to believe that an increase in the imports of foreign cars would induce the workers in the British motor industry to work harder, to moderate their fantastic wage claims, and to accept a certain degree of discipline? It does not look likely. The decline in the profits of some leading British car firms as a result of the fiercer competition by their foreign rivals in the home market has failed to affect the attitude of their workers.

Admittedly, while the removal of the tariff wall would facilitate the import of foreign cars to Britain, it would also facilitate the export of British cars to the Common Market. The difference is that continental motor manufacturers stand a better chance than British motor manufacturers of achieving an increase in the efficiency of their workers in face of increased British competition. Since the degree of demoralisation of workers on the Continent is even now much more moderate than in Britain, competition is more likely to produce there its beneficial effect than in Britain. On the Continent workers are more afraid of unemployment than in Britain and they are more likely to go out of their way to make an effort to enable their firms to meet increased British competition.

Employers, too, are in a better position on the Continent to increase their efficiency if they are threatened by an increased influx of British goods. Their fiscal system does not reduce their chances of ploughing back their profits into their business, and their trade unions do not resist the adoption of labour-saving equipment on terms on which their adoption is worth while. In other words, British industry is more in need of protection than continental industry, and the reciprocal removal of protection is less likely to harm it. In this respect, however, changes of policy under the Conservative Government might make a difference.

The rise in prices in Britain resulting from her entry into the Common Market, discussed in Chapter 13, is liable to encourage imports in addition to the encouragement they would receive from the removal of the tariff walls. What is just as important, the effect of the rise in prices in Britain on British wages would stimulate imports from the EEC and would handicap British exports to the EEC. According to *Britain in Europe*, published by the Confederation of British Industries, an additional increase in prices of 1 per cent is accompanied by an additional increase in wages of $1\frac{1}{2}$ per cent. Thus, if the combined effect of higher food prices and the adoption of the value-added tax were an increase in the cost of living by 8 per cent, there would be an increase in wages of 12 per cent. Even if it is spread over a period of years in the transition period, it would be sufficient to impose a noteworthy handicap on British exports – not only those to the EEC countries but also to everywhere else – and a corresponding stimulus to imports by Britain – not only from the EEC but also from everywhere else.

As pointed out in the last chapter, it is a popular fallacy to assume that any increase of exports to the EEC resulting from the removal of customs barriers by the EEC countries for British goods would be a net addition to the total of British exports. This assumption would be false even if we disregarded the losses of markets in the Commonwealth in consequence of the termination of Preferences, largely because the 'English disease' would prevent industries which stand to benefit by the change from exploiting their opportunities. Many of these industries are already working to capacity and could only increase their output if the workers abandoned their practices that keep output down. If output could only be increased through working more overtime, the higher rates of overtime pay would offset and more than offset the advantages to be gained by the elimination of the tariffs in the EEC.

Closer contact with continental workers is most unlikely to inspire British workers to increase their productive efforts. Possibly it might inspire continental workers to follow the British example. But few if any supporters of the Common Market idea would dare to admit it even to themselves, let alone argue in public, that they base their hopes on the possibility of spreading the 'English disease' abroad.

CHAPTER TEN

Free Movement of Labour and Capital

EVER since 1914 the world has been suffering from restrictions imposed on the movement of labour and capital across national frontiers. Even before the First World War there were in some countries certain restrictions on the emigration or immigration of labour, but they were negligible compared with the inter-war and post-war restrictions. As for capital it was allowed to move freely almost everywhere. It is no wonder the pre-1914 era is looked upon with nostalgia, having regard to the difficulties which have to be faced in our days in almost every country in respect of the inward or outward movements of labour and capital.

For this reason, the claim that in the Common Market there will eventually be complete freedom of movement of labour and capital is bound to appeal in a great many quarters. And it must be tempting for many people in Britain to envisage the possibility of a return to such freedom, at any rate between the countries of Western Europe, as an eventual result of joining the Common Market.

Many employers in the U.K. must feel tempted to support the system under which they would hope to be in a position to draw upon the manpower of a number of other countries. They are presumably less enthusiastic about the corollary to that change – that employers in Western Europe would also be in a position to draw upon the manpower of the U.K. But it is a widespread assumption that British workers would not be inclined to go to the Continent anyhow. This view is based on recent evidence. When during the early 'sixties some thousands of redundant aircraft workers found jobs in the Netherlands, Germany and Switzerland, most of them drifted back before long because, much to their dismay, they found that on the Continent they were expected to do a full day's work for their full day's pay. In any case, in the British Welfare State the unemployed are looked after so generously that most redundant British workers would prefer to await a favourable opening for re-employment at home rather than be uprooted for the sake of early re-employment abroad.

This is one of the reasons why employers in the U.K. find it difficult to attract British unemployed labour even from one district to another or from one industry to another. Most of the British unemployed – numbering over 600,000 at the time of writing – in so far as they are not unemployables, could easily find jobs if they were prepared to change their residence or their occupation. Since they are unwilling to do so even within the U.K. they are not likely to be keen on doing so in the EEC if and when the obstacles to their employment there should be removed.

Another reason why British labour is so inflexible within Britain lies in rehousing difficulties. It is admittedly quite a problem for British workers with families to take a job beyond a reasonable distance from their residence. The same problem would arise, of course, in most Western European countries, since housing accommodation is everywhere in short supply. Likewise, Western European workers who would want to come to Britain if Britain joined the EEC and if the barriers to movements of labour within the EEC were removed would face the same difficulties, aggravated by difficulties of local knowledge and of language. From the point of view of British workers there is ample scope for finding jobs for most of those who are willing to change residence without having to move to another country.

It is of course conceivable that by joining the Common Market Britain would be able to import labour from southern Italy, since the use of Italian labour is now restricted in Switzerland. The housing problem would not present unsurmountable difficulties, because Italian unskilled labourers would be prepared to put up with housing conditions which would not be tolerated by British workers. They would also be prepared to leave their families behind and remit to their relatives a high proportion of their earnings, which would of course constitute additional invisible imports for Britain. But there would be no need to join the EEC to enable British employers to attract Italian labour – Switzerland is not a member and has been employing a very large number of them for many years – to grant many of them visas and working permits. But this would conflict with the British policy of restraining immigration of labour from the Commonwealth and would encounter strong opposition.

Of course the removal of barriers to movements of labour would open wider possibilities for highly paid specialised labour to go where they receive the highest pay. But at that level the existing barriers to the movements of labour are little more than a mere formality. There is no diffiiculty for specialists to obtain working permits anywhere. Conceivably the removal of this formality within the EEC might induce British specialists to go abroad and foreign specialists to come to this country if the terms offered to them are sufficiently tempting. In which direction the brain-drain would operate is anybody's guess.

At the other extreme, the removal of barriers to the immigration of continental labour might induce the worst type of foreign workers to come to Britain, because of the possibility of being paid a full day's pay without having to do a full day's work. Idlers and spongers exist everywhere, but in few other countries are they pampered to the same extent as in Britain. To the idlers and spongers of Western Europe Britain might well appear as the country of their dreams, where they can draw their wages for doing the minimum amount of work, or even without doing any work at all, under terms of typically British settlements of inter-union borderline disputes, or under arrangements by which employers must keep on their payroll workers made superfluous by the adoption of more efficient methods of production. The multitude of devices of malingering – doctors under the National Health Service sign certificates without seeing the 'patient' – of go-slow, etc., are bound to attract the

parasitic type of foreign workers who find it much more difficult to get away with malpractices in their own countries.

It may well be asked whether the possibility of attracting
that type of labour as a result of joining the EEC should be
considered an item on the credit side of the proposed change
or on the debit side. In either case, the EEC is still very far
from having been able to remove all barriers to the free movement of labour, even though progress is being made in that
direction.

To business firms, investors and bankers the prospect of a
greater freedom of movement for capital is bound to sound
attractive. But in conditions prevailing at the time of writing
there are ample capital movements between the U.K. and the
EEC countries. There is a growing volume of direct investment
of German, French, Dutch, etc., capital in Britain, and British
capital has been invested in recent years on a considerable
scale in EEC countries. Much of it had to go through the investment currency market, and admittedly the high premium
on such currencies did discourage direct investment on the
Continent to a high degree, even though the Bank of England
granted licences in what it considered to be deserving cases to
transfer the capital in the ordinary way. Likewise portfolio
investments have been a two-way traffic, especially as non-
residents have been entitled during the past twenty years to
withdraw their capital provided the original investment met
with the approval of the British authorities. Now they are
entirely free to dispose of their U.K. securities and to dispose
of the sterling proceeds.

While it would have been to the advantage of investors and
of business concerns in the U.K. if capital movements had been
completely free, there can be no doubt that it would have
greatly aggravated the series of sterling crises experienced in
the 'fifties and the 'sixties. In the absence of exchange control
in all EEC countries there would have been an even larger
volume of foreign capital invested in the U.K. against which
non-resident investors would have been hedging whenever
sterling was under a cloud. And fears of a sterling devaluation

or of anti-capitalist legislation and taxation would have induced many more U.K. residents to transfer capital abroad in the absence of the restrictions that have been in operation ever since the war.

It would not be an unmitigated blessing if industries and investors in the EEC were given an absolutely free hand to invest in the U.K. and if U.K. residents were given an absolutely free hand to invest in other countries of the EEC. The needs of British industries for continental capital can be met to a high degree under the existing conditions thanks to the development of the Euro-bond market which enables credit-worthy British firms to borrow in the form of medium- and long-term bond issues in Germany, Switzerland and elsewhere. It is true, the lending countries impose limits from time to time on such issues, so that the issuing banks have to 'ration' the would-be borrowers. But it is difficult to conceive conditions in which any Government could possibly feel it could afford to remove the limits of lending even to countries in the Common Market. From this point of view membership in the Common Market would only bring a difference in degree – and not a very high degree at that. Unless and until the monetary unification of the EEC is completed, surplus countries will have to continue to take great care not to overlend abroad, whether to EEC countries or to other countries.

Nor is there any reason for being in favour of joining the Common Market for the sake of a liberalisation of transfers of short-term funds. Even in existing conditions, transfers connected with genuine commercial transactions are free and restrictions are only directed against speculative and arbitrage transactions. Would it be to Britain's interests to remove altogether such restrictions for foreign exchange transactions with EEC countries? In the absence of controls the flight of short-term funds from Britain to West Germany would have assumed landslide-like dimensions on a number of occasions in recent years. Even as it was, it was difficult for the British authorities to resist pressure due to flights into D. marks of funds held in London by non-residents. Had U.K. residents also been free to transfer their money to Frankfurt, the pressures would have become many times larger. Speculative operations, too, would have been incomparably larger in the absence of the rule restricting forward exchange transactions on account of U.K. residents to transactions connected with genuine imports and exports.

Until recently the idea of being able to obtain short-term credits where interest rates were lowest might have made many converts to joining the EEC among British businessmen affected by the credit squeeze. But in the late 'sixties the Bank of England became much more liberal in granting licences to U.K. residents for the purpose of borrowing in terms of foreign currencies. Even in the absence of a complete removal of the restrictions in relation to the EEC countries, foreign currency credits assumed such dimensions that they weakened considerably the effect of the credit squeeze. The control of the authorities over the supply of credit would become even weaker if, as a result of joining the Common Market, and as a result of a complete liberalisation of credits between EEC countries, U.K. firms were placed in a position of being able to borrow abroad or in terms of foreign currencies as a matter of routine all the funds they were prevented from borrowing in sterling at home.

In this respect, as in respect of unrestricted movements of long-term capital, most members of the Common Market could not afford to remove all barriers until the unification of their currencies were completed. From time to time surplus countries could of course afford to remove all controls. Both Germany and France were able to do so in the 'sixties. But France felt impelled to reimpose her controls in a hurry after the troubles of 1968. Premature removal of controls would make for instability and would place the financially weaker country at a grave disadvantage both within the EEC and outside it. Even financially strong countries such as Germany had to ration long-term lending abroad and discourage the influx of long-term and short-term capital.

CHAPTER ELEVEN

Monetary Unification – at a Price

IN an ideal world there would be only one currency which would be accepted in payment everywhere. Although the idea of such a Utopian system was put forward from time to time, it is outside the realm of practical politics. On the other hand, there has lately been a growing volume of speculation about the possibility of unifying the monetary systems of the EEC countries into one single Western European monetary system. The Werner Report argued that the realisation of that idea would have to be preceded by considerable progress towards the economic integration of the Common Market. There is sharp difference of opinion within the EEC on this question.

Until a few years ago the mere remote possibility that, should Britain join the Common Market, sterling might disappear as a separate monetary unit and be merged into a European currency would have been sufficient to turn a great many people against joining the Common Market. British people were rightly proud of their sterling and of its important international role, and any Government which would have agreed to an arrangement that might have led to sterling's disappearance would have incurred widespread unpopularity, not only in the City but also in the country at large. Indeed, such a possibility would have been widely deplored throughout the Sterling Area and even outside it, in many countries which had used sterling in their international trade and which had respected and admired it.

Unfortunately those days are now a matter of the past. Five years of misgovernment after 1964 were sufficient to deprive sterling of its former glamour. Apart from the frequently recurrent sterling crises and the devaluation of 1967, the fact that the Labour Government made the termination of sterling's international role its declared policy deprived sterling of much of its former prestige abroad. Even at home, after the difficulties caused by the measures adopted for its defence, a great many people would now witness its demise without regrets. Indeed the suggestion that a joint European currency would be stronger than sterling and that its defence would not call for efforts and sacrifices comparable to those demanded by the defence of sterling in 1964–69 is now considered a strong argument in favour of joining the Common Market.

It is very easy to talk about the merging of sterling, the mark, the French franc, the Belgian franc, the guilder and perhaps a number of other currencies into one single currency. I wonder how many people who talk so glibly about it have taken the trouble to consider all the implications of such a reform. Of course the subject is much too technical and too complicated for a great many advocates of the change to go into its details; they prefer to be pleasantly vague. So most of those who think that it would be a good idea fail to make it clear that its realisation would be quite impossible unless a central monetary authority were created with powers overriding those of the Governments, Parliaments and electorates of the EEC countries, and unless the economic policies of these countries were determined by the Brussels Commission, the EEC Council of Finance Ministers and/or the Strasbourg Parliament.

Those who advocate monetary unification as a means for political and economic integration are putting the cart before the horse. There could be no monetary unification unless and until a sufficient degree of political and economic integration has been achieved to make it possible to set up such a supra-national monetary authority. It would have to possess the power to determine the total volume of money and credit for the entire group of associated countries, and to allocate their respective shares in the total. General elections or Parliamentary victories or defeats would no longer decide whether the country should be governed by an inflationist Government or by a deflationist Government. All that would be decided for us in Brussels, or wherever the supra-national monetary authority would be established. Conceivably that might be a change for the better, if the new authority – for the sake of convenience we might call it the Federal Reserve Board of Europe – could be relied upon to be fair to all and to be guided solely by the interests of the entire group of countries. In that case the liberation of monetary and economic policy from local political pressures would be decidedly a step in the right direction. But are we justified in assuming that the new authority would be managed in such a spirit? It would take a great deal to resist pressures to which the Board would be subjected from this Government and that Government to influence its decision in favour of the interests of their respective countries. And even if the countries concerned had the good fortune of obtaining the services of the supermen required for fulfilling their task, would the member Governments necessarily feel bound by their rulings? Vital national economic, political and social interests would be at stake. There would be a strong temptation for Governments who would rightly or wrongly regard the Board's decisions as unfair and highly damaging to their national interests to decide that withdrawal from the organisation and even from the EEC would be the lesser of two evils between which it would be their responsibility to choose. Or their Parliaments or electorates would decide matters for them, if the countries were still democracies, so that the Governments could be replaced by another set of Ministers who would put national interests first.

At the moment the discussion of this subject is of purely academic interest. We are still very far from the stage at which politicians would have to decide for or against adopting a common currency for the Common Market. But the first step – albeit one of very limited significance – is under preparation, and quite possibly it might actually be taken in the near future. That first step will be the decision to narrow down the limits of fluctuations of exchange rates between EEC currencies. It is a purely technical measure, and its political significance lies merely in the fact that it runs against the prevailing trend that is in favour of broader ranges of fluctuations. It is meant to be a gesture indicating the intention of the Common Market to detach itself from the existing international monetary system which is in operation under the IMF rules.

It is impossible to avoid technicalities in this attempt to describe this first step towards the unification of the monetary system of the Common Market. Under the prevailing system member Governments of the International Monetary Fund are under obligation to keep the fluctuations of their currencies in relation to the U.S. dollar within 1 per cent on either side oi their fixed parities in relation to the dollar. In practice for most leading currencies the limit is fixed in the vicinity of $\frac{3}{4}$ per cent on either side of their dollar parities. That limit is officially fixed in respect of the dollar rate only. Member Governments are under obligation to prevent an appreciation or depreciation of their exchanges in relation to the dollar beyond the 'support points' – in the case of sterling it is $2.38 to $2.42 – by Central Bank intervention in the market, consisting of buying or selling dollars at the support points or at rates between them. They are under no obligation to intervene to prevent an appreciation or depreciation of exchange rates other than the dollar. But private arbitrage operations prevent these exchange rates from rising or falling beyond $1\frac{1}{2}$ per cent on either side of parities. Their range of fluctuations is in practice 3 per cent, twice as wide as that of the dollar rate which is kept within $1\frac{1}{2}$ per cent. A detailed explanation of this technical point is found in my *Textbook on Foreign Exchange*.

Rightly or wrongly a number of Central Banks and the IMF are now inclined to favour a broadening of the 'spread' between the support points of the dollar rate to 2 per cent, possibly to 3 per cent. At the time of writing it is not certain whether this will actually be done, but if it should be done it would mean that the range of fluctuations of rates between non-dollar currencies would widen to 6 per cent.

So far from agreeing to such a widening of the range, a report produced by an EEC committee declared itself in favour of narrowing the range of fluctuations of the rates between EEC currencies from 3 per cent to 2 per cent.

This could be done by intervening whenever their exchange rates tend to appreciate or depreciate beyond 1 per cent from each side of their parities, as it is done at the time of writing in respect of the dollar. But if the IMF should rule that the intervention points of the dollar rate could henceforth be $1\frac{1}{2}$ per cent on both sides of its parities, and if Central Banks availed themselves of this permission, it would mean that the range of the permissible fluctuations of the dollar would become wider than that of the permissible fluctuations of EEC currencies in relation to each other.

This technical change would create a separate EEC foreign exchange system that would differ from the system operating under the rules of the IMF. It would be a minor step towards the goal of a unified currency for the EEC. It was understood at the time of writing that the British Government was inclined to adhere to the proposed EEC exchange-rate arrangements and to narrow the range of fluctuations of sterling in relation to EEC currencies to 2 per cent, while maintaining the range of fluctuations for dollars at its present figure of $1\frac{1}{2}$ per cent, unless the IMF authorised its widening to 2 per cent or to 3 per cent and the United States authorities themselves allowed the dollar to fluctuate within that range without intervening to prevent it. This would be meant to be a gesture to show Britain's willingness to conform to the EEC system of support points. In given circumstances it might mean in the long run, should the dollar be allowed to fluctuate within a wider range, that sterling might be kept stable in relation to the EEC currencies and would fluctuate more widely in terms of the dollar. To appreciate the significance of such a situation it must be borne in mind that, from the point of view of sterling and of British trade, the dollar is more important than all the EEC currencies taken together.

It is conceivable that the EEC might decide to narrow the spread between the support points of their currencies in relation to each other even further, and that the ultimate end is for EEC Central Banks to buy and sell each others' currencies at their parities. Such a degree of rigidity would be without precedent. Even under the gold standard there was a spread between the

gold points. But it would be a technical step towards the unification of the EEC currencies, with or without the participation
of sterling in the arrangement.

The next step towards the unification of EEC currencies
would be the abolition of exchange restrictions between EEC
countries. Although progress was made in that direction during
the 'sixties – West Germany and, for a short time also, France
removed all exchange controls – the French crisis of 1968 and
the flight to the D. mark culminating in its revaluation in 1969
brought about a set-back. Even West Germany had to adopt
restrictive measures, not against a flight of capital but against
an unwanted influx of capital. It would be some time before
progress towards integration could overcome this hurdle.

Should this be achieved, and should Britain join the Common
Market, it would mean that sterling would be exposed to heavy
selling pressure whenever there is a flight of capital to some
other EEC country. At present sterling is safeguarded to some
extent by a number of restrictive measures affecting mainly
capital transactions but also current transactions. These
measures are reinforced whenever there is a sterling scare. It
is easy to imagine how much heavier selling pressure on sterling
would have been on a number of occasions in recent years if
U.K. residents had been free to transfer their money to West
Germany or France or one of the other EEC countries.

Admittedly, under existing arrangements EEC countries
which are in trouble are permitted to adopt emergency measures
which involve a reinforcement of exchange restrictions in relation to other EEC countries. Presumably the same rule would
continue to operate also after a complete removal of exchange
control within the EEC. Judging by the extent to which the
'English disease' has become aggravated during 1970 it would
be unduly optimistic to hope that, should Britain join the
Common Market within the next few years, sterling would be
sufficiently strong and safe to face the risk of removing exchange
control in relation to the other EEC countries. In all probability it would have to be reimposed almost immediately, in
the same way as its convertibility had to be suspended in a

matter of weeks after it was restored in 1947. This would not strengthen the position and prestige of Britain within the Common Market.

But the narrowing of fluctuations of EEC currencies and the removal of exchange controls between them would only be pre-liminary steps towards monetary unification. After all, that stage was reached by the Sterling Area many years ago, and yet members of the Sterling Area retained their independent monetary units and their independent monetary policies. A much more important and much more difficult step would be the replacement of the national currencies by a common Western European currency which would be legal tender throughout the EEC. As pointed out earlier in this chapter, this would necessitate the setting-up of an authority which would allocate the currency and credit between the member countries and which would impose its policy on the Govern-ments of the member countries.

It is highly doubtful whether it would be found feasible to apply the American Federal Reserve system to Europe. Admit-tedly, the interests of various Federal Reserve Districts may be conflicting and some Federal Reserve Banks are inclined at times to take an independent line. There is always grumbling in the Middle West and parts of the West and the South that their interests are given a low priority by those who determine monetary and economic policies. But the conflict of interest could never be so sharp between States of a well-established and very gradually developed federation as between inde-pendent European national States with long traditions of inde-pendence. Since the outcome of the American Civil War nobody in the United States thinks in terms of the possibility of seceding from the Union. It is taken for granted that the fifty States are bound together for better or for worse. Even if the various European nationalities were as intermingled as those in the United States, it would take two centuries of co-existence within the Common Market before such a spirit could develop in Western Europe. The possibility of breaking away would re-main for a long time, and its existence would limit the extent to which a central authority would be in a position to impose its policies on member countries.

For this reason alone the idea of a united Western European currency must be regarded as Utopian. Enthusiastic advocates of joining the Common Market who argue that it would lead to a unification of the Western European monetary system misjudge their public if they think that, by misleading them into believing in that possibility, they would increase the number of those in favour of joining. The proportion of people in Britain who would be prepared to relinquish national sovereignty to the extent required by the establishment and operation of a common currency must be infinitesimal.

Another objection to joining the proposed EEC monetary system even at its initial stages is that as a result of its application the dollar would cease to be the sole intervention currency – that is, the currency used by all Central Banks to intervene when their exchange rates tend to go beyond support points. This again is a rather technical point but it is essential to consider it because of its broader implications. If the official support points of the sterling–D. mark rate were fixed at 1 per cent on each side of its parity, while the official support points of the sterling–dollar rate were widened to $1\frac{1}{2}$ per cent on each side of its parity, then the dollar could no longer be used by the Bank of England for preventing sterling from deviating from its parity with the D. mark beyond $\frac{3}{4}$ per cent on each side. It would be necessary to use the D. mark as intervention currency instead of the dollar. Otherwise the dollar would be kept closer to its parity than the American authorities would want it to be kept. The same applies to all exchange rates between EEC currencies and between them and sterling if Britain should join the arrangement. The whole burden of maintaining the dollar might possibly fall on the Central Banks of the EEC countries. To avoid this, the Central Banks would only intervene with the end of each others' currencies. They would only use dollars if the premium or the discount on the dollar tended to go beyond $1\frac{1}{2}$ per cent.

As a result the need for holding dollars for the purpose of

intervention would diminish considerably. This would constitute an additional reason for EEC Central Banks to press for the conversion of their dollars into gold or into some other currencies, to the detriment of the dollar. In view of the importance of avoiding any action which might weaken the position of the dollar and of the United States in the interests of the free world, the narrowing of the spreads between EEC currencies would be ill-advised, and it would be ill-advised for Britain to join such an arrangement. On the other hand, it would be equally ill-advised for the United States and for the International Monetary Fund to assume responsibility for such a split in the international monetary front by widening the spread, having regard to the strong feeling against such widening in the EEC.

In so far as the unification of the EEC currencies would tend to discourage the IMF and the United States from adopting wider spreads or any other forms of increased flexibility, it would render a useful service to the cause of international monetary stability. But since a detachment of EEC currencies from the dollar would be yet another manifestation of EEC anti-Americanism, Britain should have nothing to do with it.

CHAPTER TWELVE

The Costs of Joining

WE have now examined the principal claims made by those in favour of joining the Common Market about the alleged advantages Britain would gain from becoming a member of the EEC. I sought to prove that it would not be worth our while to join for the sake of the highly problematic political and military advantages our membership would secure. I argued that closer economic association with Western Europe would not add to the deterrent provided by our military association in NATO, and might weaken it if it were to lead to disengagement by the United States. My further point was that Britain's membership in the Common Market, so far from reinforcing our existing friendly relationship, would be liable to produce the opposite effect because of the clashes of vital economic interests that are liable to arise from our closer association. I further sought to show that the case for joining the Common Market for the sake of the advantages of a larger market, the possibility of creating bigger firms, and the increased extent of free competition, are grossly overrated. So are the advantages of a free movement of labour and capital. Another claim I sought to dispose of was that membership in the EEC would solve our balance of payments problem or would cure the 'English disease'. Finally I criticised as Utopian the idea of monetary integration culminating in the creation of a unified European currency.

But even if all the claims put forward in favour of joining the EEC were justified, there would still remain the question whether the disadvantages that would result from it would not amount to an excessive price to be paid for all the advantages we could possibly derive from it. And even if the estimated benefits were certain to compensate us, and more than compensate us, for the sacrifices involved, is Britain likely to be in a position to pay the price? It is not merely a question whether we would get full value for our money, but also whether we can afford to pay the money. Admittedly, it is the prevailing fashion to embark on promising schemes which pay in the long run and trust to luck that we shall be in a position to pay the costs. But in this instance the cost is so gigantic that it is our duty to consider whether it would be within our means, apart altogether from the question whether it would be worth our while to pay it.

Many supporters of the policy in favour of joining the Common Market are at pains to emphasise that there is a limit beyond which the price to be paid for our admission would be too high. In many instances that is plain lip-service paid for considerations of expediency. Some enthusiasts of joining the Common Market would be quite prepared to sign on the dotted line of the Treaty of Rome plus all the subsequent agreements and would be willing to agree to a very short transition period. But they are aware that they would encounter unsurmountable opposition in British public opinion, and even party discipline in Parliament might be put under a rather severe strain by an unconditional surrender to the EEC terms. So they are prepared to go through the gestures of a stiff fight to secure concessions, especially in the form of a longer transition period. It is easier to obtain grudging consent for the sacrifices if they are not due to be made for some years to come, at any rate not to anything like their full extent. People are apt to forget how quickly a transition period of three years or even of five years is apt to pass.

It is an oft-repeated argument of those in favour of joining that they are at a disadvantage, because the price to be paid for membership is concrete and obvious, while the advantages are abstract, difficult to prove and are liable to materialise to anything like their full extent in the long run only. The latter argument should not by itself influence our judgement unduly. Opponents of the Common Market idea should not rely too much on Keynes's much-quoted remark: 'In the long run we are all dead.' I am quite certain that it was a wisecrack Keynes made in a whimsical mood and that he never intended it to be regarded as the enunciation of the principle that only short-run considerations matter. In the course of our lives we all have to choose on many occasions between short-run and long-run considerations, in our professional or business life as well as in our private life. As often as not most of us are likely to strike a compromise between the two. So if only we were certain that the price to be paid for our admission would not be excessive and we could afford to pay it, the fact that the benefits would only accrue in the long run should not deter us from deciding in favour of joining. But the decision must be taken with our eyes wide open about the extent of the cost and about the degree of uncertainty of the beneficial results.

As already pointed out, the extent of the benefits is difficult to estimate and our estimates of them depend largely on our attitude towards free-trade ideology. Those who believe in the all-curing effects of wider trading areas and of keener competition, and who accept the forecast that the future belongs to the gigantic firms, are inclined to value the benefits very high. They are unable, however, to quantify their estimates of the benefits for the sake of convincing those who do not share their quasi-religious faith.

Nor is it easy, for that matter, to estimate the costs of joining the Common Market even with approximate accuracy. The Labour Government sought to solve the problem by issuing a White Paper in February 1970 giving maximum and minimum estimates for all items. The gap between them was in many instances so wide that the exercise merely proved the impossibility of counting the costs. What is one to think of the statement of the White Paper that estimates of the cost of entry alone, as distinct from current costs once we are in the EEC, vary between £100 million and £1,100 million? Even these extreme limits were given subject to reservations.

I cannot help suspecting that, by the beginning of 1970, Mr Wilson and his colleagues were having second thoughts about the wisdom of their earlier display of enthusiasm for joining the

EEC, an attitude which had conveyed the impression that, if only France waived her veto, Britain would be willing and eager to join regardless of the costs. The election was approaching and it might have appeared expedient to let it be understood that the Government was in fact counting the costs before coming to a definite decision. Otherwise the Government would not have released a White Paper which gave prohibitive maximum figures, and this at a time before the Government could possibly be certain whether the improvement in the balance of payments was of a lasting character. The mere possibility of having to find £1,100 million at a time when the figures of Britain's external short-term indebtedness were of near-astronomic magnitude was sufficient for the Government to damp down its enthusiasm, and that of some others, for joining the Common Market at all costs.

Difficult as it is to estimate the costs, their conflicting estimates are based on more realistic considerations than the hopes of benefits that supporters of the EEC policy entertain, largely through wishful thinking. Yet it would be essential to prove the likelihood of substantial benefits and to give some idea about their extent in order to make the sacrifice appear to be worth while. For even if the extent of the costs should prove to be only half-way between the maximum and minimum estimates of the White Paper, they would be formidable, and to incur such liabilities would constitute a gamble which Britain could ill afford. The White Paper is confined to estimates of the burden on the balance of payments, the British contribution to the Community's budget and the Common Agricultural policy. But there are bound to be innumerable items of costs which are outside the scope of the White Paper. Their extent would be fully as uncertain as the extent of benefits.

Who would be bold enough to venture a forecast of the cost of the losses of many business firms resulting from the fundamental change? Any such change is bound to benefit a number of firms and is bound to inflict losses on a number of other firms. In a great many instances the extent of such losses would be liable to be so large that it would bankrupt the firms, wiping out a high proportion of their owners' capital. If a factory had to close down because it was unable to survive increased competition from the Common Market, the resulting loss would represent a very high percentage of the capital invested in it. On the other hand, if another factory of equal size were to do better because it was able to compete successfully in the Common Market, the chances are that its additional profits would offset a mere fraction of the first factory's capital loss. So the chances are that on balance losses would exceed profits considerably.

Before discussing the potential costs in detail in the following chapters, it is necessary to point out the immeasurable disadvantage of the high degree of uncertainty created by the prolonged negotiations for entering the Common Market. Nobody can be certain whether these negotiations will be successful and, if so, on what terms Britain would be admitted. Nobody can have even a vague idea how he, or his firm, would be affected by the change. Since negotiations are likely to drag on for years – the projected dateline for our entry is 1973 – and since during the period of transition the full extent of the favourable or unfavourable effects of the agreement would not become evident for a long time, the period of uncertainty is likely to continue for a long time, something between six and nine years. Meanwhile everybody, or almost everybody, will be kept in uncertainty about the way he is likely to be affected as a businessman, an employee, a shareholder or a consumer. Capital plans are liable to be deferred, for it is hardly worth while expanding a plant, in spite of the current demand for goods, if there is more than a bare possibility that the demand might dry up as a result of an influx of cheaper continental goods a few years hence, before the capital expenditure on expansion could be written off.

During the negotiations and the period of transition, and for another year or two until the full effect of the change becomes evident, the sword of Damocles will be pending over the heads of many millions of people in Britain. The psychological effects of this prolonged uncertainty, and its effect on planning ahead, must be added to the costs in terms of human happiness and prosperity.

Even the Heath Government, which is enthusiastic about joining the Common Market, readily admits that the direct costs would be exorbitant and unfair. In July 1970 it submitted a paper to the Brussels Commission estimating the British contribution to the EEC at 31 per cent of the EEC budget by 1978, even though Britain's national income would represent only 17 per cent of the total national income of the enlarged EEC. We are expected to buy our way into the EEC by assuming a disproportionate share of the burden. According to British official calculations, during the first year after the end of the transition period Britain would be out of pocket to the extent of £468 million, while during the same year France would benefit to the extent of £319 million. Even allowing for the impossibility of claiming any degree of accuracy for such advance estimates, the basic fact that the British taxpayer would have to subsidise the French farmer through the operation of the Common Agricultural Policy is incontestable. The amount of that subsidy would exceed considerably the subsidies paid by the British taxpayer to British farmers for the sake of keeping down the price of goods. If we joined the Common Market we would have to pay higher farm subsidies without getting the benefit of lower prices.

Needless to say, the EEC has contested the British figures and the negotiations are likely to be largely about the accuracy of the conflicting 'guesstimates'. Would the British Government join the Common Market on the basis of its own estimates of 1970 of the probable cost? Or would it only be prepared to join if the EEC should be willing to make concessions which would reduce those costs? If Britain is keener, and shows herself keener, to join than the EEC is to admit her, her bargaining position would be very weak. The Government would then pretend to have allowed itself to be convinced that, after all, its estimates of 1970 were excessive. But the critics of its policy at General Elections would always quote against it the figures to which it lent its authority at the beginning of the negotiations.

Would Britain be in a position in 1978 to contribute nearly £500 million to the EEC's budget? Would she have a balance of payments surplus of that magnitude? It is utterly impossible to foresee what her position will be in eight years' time. No responsible Government could possibly assume such a commitment. Britain would be simply unable to afford it.

It may be argued that the incalculable advantages derived from joining would offset, and more than offset, such a direct cost. Against this we must also take into consideration the incalculable disadvantages. The following three chapters will deal with the disadvantages to be derived from the rise in prices and from sacrificing Britain's special relationship with the Commonwealth and with the United States. But there are many other obvious though incalculable disadvantages. For instance, joining the Common Market would entail the reduction and possibly the eclipse of London's role as an international financial centre, insurance centre and commercial centre. The invisible exports derived from these and other functions, which are estimated at hundreds of millions per annum, would decline very considerably.

CHAPTER THIRTEEN

Deliberate Increase of Prices

EVEN the most fanatical advocates of joining the Common Market admit, however reluctantly, that it would mean a substantial increase in the cost of living. Yet, knowing this, they nevertheless favour a policy that is bound to accentuate the rising trend in prices, even though they have been escalating already at an alarming rate lately. During a period of a declining trend in prices, such as the world experienced most of the time between the wars, the effect of joining the EEC would be offset by the general downward trend. Even during a period of stable prices the extent of its effect might be acceptable. But it would be an unpardonable degree of short-sightedness to take deliberate action to cause a substantial extra rise in prices amidst a period of creeping but escalating inflation.

Given the existing inflationary wage–price spiral, the additional rise in prices, wages and costs to be caused by joining the Common Market is bound to be self-aggravating. By the look of things the development of a galloping inflation seems to be in any case a mere question of time. But why, in the name of reason, adopt a policy which would bring us even nearer to the phase of runaway inflation? Surely the sensible attitude would be to fight a stubborn rearguard action against the process of inflation, to gain time in the remote hope that something might happen to halt it before it assumes disastrous dimensions.

Instead, both major political parties have committed themselves, in their wisdom, to joining the Common Market, in the certain knowledge that it would step up the pace of non-stop inflation. Political pressure coming from all sides encourages the Government to take the fateful step that would greatly reduce our hopes – at any rate the hopes of the older generation –

that somehow the climax of inflation when prices will double overnight as they did in Germany in 1923 would not be reached in our lifetime.

There are two ways in which joining the Common Market would produce an inflationary effect. It would raise the price of food in Britain and, in consequence, the cost of production and the general price level. And it would lead to the adoption of the value-added tax. Of course it seems possible that the Conservative Government, for the sake of reducing direct taxation, would adopt that tax anyhow. But the idea that the adoption of that tax would bring Britain a step nearer to economic integration with the EEC will doubtless play an important part in finalising the decision to adopt a tax which is bound to raise the cost of living.

By joining the Common Market Britain would abandon her traditional policy of keeping down food prices. She would abandon her basic principle that essential consumer goods should be bought where they are produced at the lowest cost. Ever since the adoption of the Anti-Corn Law Act, British industry had the advantage of low-priced imported food, thanks to which wages were relatively low and manufactures tended to remain competitive. Even during the orgy of wage increases in the 'sixties and in 1970 it was possible to keep down the cost of living and the cost of production to some extent. But now the Government intends to abandon this advantage deliberately and allow the prices of British agricultural products to adjust themselves to the high price level of Western European producers. For the sake of being admitted into the EEC, import duties are imposed on food imported from the Commonwealth and from other overseas countries. The British housewife will have to pay the high prices based on high production costs of inefficient Western European farmers.

This will provide an additional excuse for trade unions to step up their wage demands. Higher food prices will lead to higher costs of manufactured goods for the home consumer, which again will lead to even higher wage demands. The relative advantage enjoyed by British exporters would disappear and the balance of payments would be affected accordingly. A further handicap would be imposed on British exports both to the EEC and to other countries.

The extent of this increase in the cost of food and its effect is of course no matter of simple arithmetic. All calculations are based on the present level of Western European farm prices. But there is no reason for assuming that those prices would remain static. Once Britain has burnt her boats there would be nothing to prevent her partners in the EEC ganging together to raise the level of farm prices even higher and to widen the differential between them and world prices. The withdrawal of subsidies and deficiency payments to British farmers would mean a steep rise in home-produced farm-product prices more or less to the level of the corresponding products of Western European countries.

The exclusion of agricultural products of countries outside the EEC from the British market would tend to lower their world prices outside the EEC. This would mean that our industrial rivals outside the EEC would be able to keep down wages and costs of production, and their relative competitive capacity would increase.

Another way in which the cost of living is intended to be raised deliberately is through the adoption of the value-added tax. Although to some extent it will replace the existing purchase tax, it will cover the whole range of goods and services and will raise the cost of living with a stroke of the pen, at the same time as the prices of agricultural products are also raised. The combined effect of these two increases is bound to be considerable. While it may be understandable if many people would like to adopt the value-added tax in isolation, for the sake of cutting direct taxation – especially for the sake of getting rid of the Selective Employment Tax, the stupidest tax since the abolition of the tax on windows – it is impossible to find any justification for making its adoption simultaneously with the increase in the cost of living as a result of the abandonment of the policy of cheap food.

But there can be other objections to the value-added tax

besides its direct effect on prices. The basic principle of switching from direct to indirect taxation is liable to give rise to strong resentment among the classes which are unable to pass on the additional burden to the consumer by demanding and obtaining higher wages. While the higher food prices resulting from joining the Common Market are an effect that is incidental to a policy action by the Government, the increase of prices caused by the new fiscal measures is a direct Government measure calculated to protect the higher income groups at the expense of the lower income groups.

Without being a dogmatic egalitarian – indeed I feel that during the post-war period egalitarianism has been grossly overdone – I doubt if it would be possible to put the clock back. The most one may reasonably expect is to check the trend which is in existing conditions detrimental to productivity and contributes therefore towards slowing down the increase of the standard of living of the lower income groups. But to try to shift back the burden of taxation on those who can afford it least would be a retrograde step which would generate widespread resentment. It would be bad enough to let prices rise through raising the prices of land products to the high level prevailing in Western Europe. It would be a great deal worse to make prices rise deliberately through fiscal action.

There is everything to be said for encouraging saving and for giving corporations and individuals a better chance to retain and reinvest the amounts saved instead of applying confiscatory taxation. That end could be achieved by lowering Corporation Tax and surtax. But it would be difficult to make such measures widely acceptable by those who do not benefit by them directly if such tax cuts were to coincide with measures calculated to increase the burden of indirect taxation on necessities. The discontent arising from other effects of joining the Common Market would be greatly aggravated by the effect of the value-added tax. Of course, quite possibly the value-added tax will be adopted long before we join the EEC, and even if we should be unable to join it.

According to the White Paper on *Britain and the European*

Communities: An Economic Assessment (Cmnd 4289), the increase in the retail price index for food resulting from joining the Common Market might be of the order of 18 to 26 per cent, which would cause an increase in the cost of living index of 4 to 5 per cent. This may appear moderate, considering that for years the cost of living was increasing at about that rate and more recently its increase was accelerating considerably. But we must bear in mind that for lower income groups food prices represent a higher proportion of their spendings than for medium and higher income groups. This means that for the old-age pensioner and for other victims of inflation this additional increase in food prices by 18–26 per cent would result in an increase in the cost of living far in excess of the 4–5 per cent estimated by Government statisticians.

Nor is the argument of the White Paper that this rise would be spread over a period of years and its full effect felt only at the end of the transition period very comforting. For one thing, it is well on the cards that the Government, for the sake of being admitted, will eventually consent to a brief transition period. Moreover, the effect of value-added and food tax tax would be immediate, and the self-aggravating effect of the resulting rise in the cost of living would exaggerate the effect of the increase in food prices. The certainty of the all-round increase in prices resulting from joining the Common Market would tend to induce many people to anticipate their purchases and to hedge against the certain increase.

As the White Paper rightly says, the effect of higher food prices 'would be associated with all the other various factors which normally influence the cost of living'. The fact that there would be other factors besides the effect of joining the Common Market which would tend to cause prices to rise, would not mitigate its effect, it would only make it less obvious, which is small comfort for those who have to bear its burden. In any case the effect of value-added tax would be quite clear and unmistakable.

Supporters of the Common Market express pious hopes that, as a result of joining the EEC, distributive margins might narrow. It is odd that the Confederation of British Industries should lend its authority to such speculation which utterly lacks any realisitc foundations. Nor is the argument that quite conceivably the discrepancy between food prices within and outside the EEC might narrow more impressive. Quite possibly the change might be in exactly the opposite sense. Under the protection of the external tariff wall distributive margins and price differentials might well widen. I am not saying that they necessarily would, but the possibility is there and should not be ignored by wishful thinkers.

Actually the British housewife is beginning to pay the price for joining the Common Market even before joining. On 27 October Mr Barber announced the Government's decision to impose duties on certain food imports, in the full knowledge that this must mean higher food prices. In taking this step right at the beginning of his negotiations with the EEC the Government has discarded its principal bargaining counter without receiving any *quid pro quo* in the form of some concession of comparable importance. Years before Britain begins to derive such benefits as she might derive from her membership, the British consumer will pay the price in the form of a higher cost of living.

CHAPTER FOURTEEN

Must We Jettison the Commonwealth?

THE preceding chapters endeavoured to prove that joining the Common Market would entail some grave disadvantages, such as a substantial rise in prices and costs, a deterioration of the balance of payments and an increase in Britain's external indebtedness. But to my mind the most important argument against joining the Common Market is the effect it would produce on Britain's relationship with the United States and with certain countries of the Commonwealth. We propose to deal with the effect on what is left of the Anglo-American 'special relationship' in Chapter 15. The present chapter will try to indicate what Britain stands to lose by jettisoning the Commonwealth.

Admittedly, Britain's links with the Commonwealth have weakened considerably during the last decade or two. It is easy for advocates of the Common Market to produce statistics to show that our trade with the Commonwealth now represents a much smaller proportion of our total trade than it did in the old days. To a large degree we have only ourselves to blame for this. Instead of endeavouring to tighten our economic and political relationships at least with the former Dominions, we allowed them to weaken. Indeed from the moment Britain began to flirt with the EEC she provided the British countries overseas with every justification for an economic and political reorientation without awaiting the outcome of our negotiations. The mere possibility that the mother country might jettison Australia and New Zealand made it essential for them to forge stronger links with the United States, the country towards which they would have to turn once they are no longer in a position to rely on Britain either for trade or for defence.

Even before the Labour Government decided in favour of terminating our 'East of Suez' military commitments, the decline of the British naval and military power under Conservative as well as Socialist rule made it evident to Australia and New Zealand that Britain would no longer be in a position to protect them in case of need. The inevitable consequence has been reorientation in various ways towards the United States. This tendency received powerful stimulus when the Conservative Government declared its intention of joining the Common Market. From the very first it was evident that this would mean the end of Commonwealth Preference and the virtual exclusion, or at any rate drastic reduction, of vital Commonwealth exports to the United Kingdom. Although the prospects of Britain's admission in the EEC had their ups and downs, the intention was there all the time, apart from the Labour Party's victory in 1964 and Mr Wilson's conversion in 1966. It became necessary for Australia, New Zealand and Canada to expect that they might find themselves abandoned by Britain one day.

In the circumstances it is most remarkable that the three countries have not decided long before now to become the 51st, 52nd and 53rd States of the United States. They would have been welcomed with open arms. Of course as far as Canada is concerned, she is already virtually part of the United States from an economic point of view. This has been causing growing concern, and Canada would have responded favourably to any British effort to recover lost ground. But now that Canada as well as Australia and New Zealand have to envisage a situation in which they would have to look mainly towards the United States for their national security and prosperity, there must be a strong temptation for them to take the initiative for severing their remaining links with Britain instead of waiting until Britain actually sacrifices them to her declared policy of becoming an integral part of Western Europe. The same applies to the former British colonies in the West Indies. The fact that these former Dominions and colonies have still been endeavouring to maintain special relationships with Britain shows that there must still exist very strong sentimental links with her, in addition to their weakening trade links.

Admittedly there has been no evidence of much effort, if any, on the part of most of these countries to intensify their trade relations with Britain. But since Britain's first application for membership of the EEC there has been every economic and political reason for them to abstain from doing so. They must have realised that their future does not lie with Britain. Even before the British efforts to join the Common Market and before the policy of abandoning our 'East of Suez' commitments, it must have been evident to observers in overseas countries that Britain's financial, economic, political and military power was on the decline. Even under Conservative Governments there was a distinct tendency to sacrifice military strength for the sake of having a good time. This tendency escalated greatly under the Labour Government of 1964–70. There was very little inducement for Commonwealth countries to tie their canoes to what might well appeared to them to be a slowly sinking ship. For this reason among others, there was very little effort on the part of the Commonwealth to try to counteract the pressure in favour of severing Britain's links with the Commonwealth for the sake of joining the Common Market.

Owing to Britain's perennial sterling troubles, London's role as the financial centre of the Commonwealth and the provider of capital declined considerably even before the advent of the Labour Government. Australia and New Zealand abandoned the pound and adopted the dollar as their monetary unit. They came to conduct their foreign trade increasingly in terms of dollars instead of sterling. New York became their main capital market, and after the American balance of payments deficit made borrowing there difficult, the former Dominions came to issue loans in the Euro-bond market, mostly in terms of dollars. All the time the proportion of their trade with Britain was declining.

Although the Commonwealth countries remained members of the Sterling Area, they insisted on a certain degree of diversification of their reserves instead of keeping them all in sterling.

To check the withdrawals of Sterling Area balances, an agreement was concluded in Basle in 1968 under which a large part of them was guaranteed against a depreciation of sterling in terms of dollars. The fact that such a guarantee was deemed necessary was a hard blow to sterling's international standing and also to Commonwealth economic unity.

The short-sighted policy adopted by Britain on the occasion of the devaluation of sterling in 1967 – the most scandalously mismanaged devaluation in monetary history – also went a long way towards accelerating the disintegration of the Commonwealth. On previous occasions, in 1931 and 1949, most Commonwealth exchange rates followed sterling as a matter of course. In 1967, the British Government succeeded in dissuading most Commonwealth Governments from devaluing their currencies in sympathy with sterling. This was done for the sake of increasing the favourable short-run effect of the devaluation on the British balance of payments. But this result was achieved at the cost of sacrificing the permanent benefits derived from the united monetary front of the Commonwealth.

Since the EEC took the view that Britain could not be admitted so long as sterling was a reserve currency, it became the official policy to divest sterling deliberately of its international role. Nevertheless, the improvement of the British balance of payments was followed by a heavy influx of sterling balances from the Commonwealth and also from other parts of the Sterling Area.

One of the reasons why official circles and a section of British opinion became ready and even eager to give up Britain's special relationship with the Commonwealth was that a number of Commonwealth countries, once they had achieved their independence, became a liability rather than an asset from a political and financial point of view They expected, demanded and obtained very substantial financial assistance, far beyond Britain's reduced means. What was worse, they showed very little appreciation of these generous sacrifices, let alone gratitude for them. Indeed some of them deemed it their sacred right to spit at the hand that fed them, before, during and after feeding.

Their treatment of the British people who remained behind after they became independent left much to be desired, and the treatment of much of the British capital and enterprise in these countries was considerably less than fair.

This attitude on the part of peoples which, having been underdogs until quite recently, suddenly found themselves in the position of top dogs, was quite understandable. But so was the reaction to it in Britain, where many people arrived at the conclusion that the Commonwealth was really more trouble and expense than it was worth, and that it would be to our interests to sacrifice our special relationship with Commonwealth countries for the sake of gaining admission into the Common Market.

Those who think on such lines are of course in a position to quote many instances in support of their argument. But they overlook the fact that many Commonwealth countries still represent immense actual or potential assets. There are the old Dominions, there is Malaysia, Singapore and the West Indies.

Australia alone, with her newly discovered mineral resources, represents an immense market for British products. In the Preface I referred to the Australian Supplement published by *The Economist* on 22 August 1970, stating that Australia had the potentialities of a second United States. Even if this was a mild exaggeration, there is enough truth in it to make us think twice before jettisoning our special relationship with Australia. Beyond doubt the recent discoveries of immense mineral deposits, and those which are certain to follow, will attract many millions of immigrants, so that within a decade or two Australia is certain to become a country of considerable economic and political importance. Britain's close association with her would greatly assist in this development, at the same time as assisting Britain in retaining her status as a power with important interests far beyond the confines of Europe.

Instead, the British Government aims at sacrificing that close association for the sake of joining the Common Market. What is perhaps even more unpardonable, there is still a 'voluntary restraint' on the export of British capital to Australia, while

Britain is actively negotiating with Soviet Russia to assist her industrialisation with the aid of long-term credits totalling over £500 million. Such an amount would go a very long way towards enabling Australia to exploit her natural resources. But Britain prefers to finance the development of a potential enemy country which even in time of peace is doing its worst to undermine the British economy and misses no opportunity for making trouble in Britain and in the free world by every means at its disposal.

If instead of trying to appease an implacable enemy, Britain devoted her resources to assisting Australia in her development, it would be greatly to the advantage of both countries. It is possible to envisage an expansion of Australia that would raise her to equality with Britain in the world economy and in world politics in the course of time. Close association between the two countries, and with some other Commonwealth countries, would create an economic and political unit which would bear comparison with the present giants, the United States and the Soviet Union, and certainly with an integrated Western Europe.

Should Britain decide to become a minority member of the EEC, it would mean giving up any hope of ever recovering British national greatness. From having been a world power for centuries, comparable to ancient Rome, she would become an offshore island of Europe depending on the political and economic stability and dubious goodwill of a group of countries which is liable to disintegrate at any moment and in which her influence would be liable to be reduced to nought whenever France and Germany joined forces against her policies.

Australia and New Zealand have already gone a long way towards drifting into the political sphere of influence of the United States and into the economic sphere of influence of Japan. Should Britain join the Common Market, progress in that direction would soon be completed. And should the Common Market disintegrate sooner or later, it would then be too late for Britain to try to fall back upon the Commonwealth, as the Commonwealth would no longer exist.

It cannot be emphasised sufficiently that the damage caused

to Britain by mistaken policy would in this respect be absolutely irreparable. Any adverse effects on Britain by more Socialist misgovernment might be put right, given timely realisation by the electorate that a change of government was called for, and given a revival of the national willpower to repair the damage. But once we have lost Australia and the other loyal Commonwealth countries we have lost them for ever, in the same way as misgovernment lost America for Britain two centuries ago.

It is to be hoped that the Commonwealth countries, having realised the danger of losing their links with Britain, might make an eleventh-hour attempt to offer Britain advantages which might strengthen British opinion against joining the Common Market at the cost of losing the Commonwealth. They would in all probability respond favourably to a serious British attempt at reinforcing the links instead of severing them. More will be said about this in the concluding chapter. But at the time of writing the chances of an eleventh-hour *rapprochement* do not seem to be bright. The premature concessions made by the British Government to the EEC in the form of imposing duties on food imports, including those from the Commonwealth, are not likely to encourage the Commonwealth Governments to attempt such a *rapprochement*. Yet even now Australians and New Zealanders, among others, are very strongly pro-British. Apart altogether from commercial considerations, they would hate to sever their links with the Old Country. But it seems that the British Government does not even put up a fight to secure for these countries the status of associate which was conceded by the EEC to the remaining British colonies with the exception of Hong Kong.

CHAPTER FIFTEEN

Driving the United States into Isolation

ONE of the most deplorable effects of Britain's adhesion to the Common Market would be that it would weaken further the special relationship between the United States and Britain. Admittedly that special relationship has long ceased to be anything like as close as it was during the two world wars and for some time also in time of peace. But there is still enough left of it to be well worth preserving and, if possible, intensifying. It is certainly incorrect, or at any rate premature, to assume, just for the sake of strengthening the case for joining the EEC, that the special relationship between the two leading Anglo-Saxon countries is now entirely a matter of the past. All Common Marketeers in Britain are not anti-American, but a great many of them are. They indulge in wishful thinking by pretending that Britain could no longer rely on her special relationship with the United States.

Admittedly, the relationship between the British and American nations has always been a love–hate one. The Americans resented British arrogance, the British resented American boastfulness, to mention only those characteristics that constituted constant irritants detrimental to the special relationship. The prolonged presence of a large number of Americans in Britain during the Second World War did not help towards a better understanding between the two peoples, and it did not improve the special relationship at a lower level, in spite of the closer Anglo-American association at the highest level.

Nevertheless, the special relationship was, and still is, deeply rooted, thanks largely to the common language. Even though the majority of Americans are now no longer of Anglo-Saxon descent, the use of the English language binds them together and it binds them to Britain. So does a common literary heritage and common early history. Similarities between their legal systems and their systems of Parliamentary democracy far exceed differences between them. The same is true even concerning their basic national characteristics – if we disregard new or relatively new immigrants. In spite of the geographical distance, Britain is still nearer to the United States than to the countries of Western Europe.

Last but by no means least, now that British people realise and freely admit that they are the junior partners in the English-speaking world in spite of their historical seniority, one of the main obstacles to really close relationship has ceased.

Even so, it would be sheer self-deception not to admit that the 'special relationship' is wearing thin – that in fact it *has* worn thin. This is largely because for a long time it has operated in too one-sided a way. Britain has been for a very long time on the receiving end and America on the giving end. Owing to the deterioration of the British character since the war, Britain has assumed the role of the poor relation and the United States is getting bored with helping her again and again. Nor are her resources available for that purpose as large as before.

The policy of successive British Governments of joining the EEC has been one of the main causes of the weakening of the Anglo-American special relationship. This may sound absurd in the light of the fact that for a long time, until comparatively recently, the United States Government was doing its utmost to induce the British Government to join the Common Market.

This attitude may be explained on two grounds. For a long time after the Second World War Western Europe was very weak in a military as well as an economic sense, and it was thought in Washington that if only Britain joined the Common Market it would gain in strength. But there is good reason to believe that subconsciously the American politicians and administrators who pressed their British opposite numbers to join the Common Market, and American public opinion that was in favour of that move, were influenced by a totally different consideration. Writing in the *Commercial and Financial Chronicle* of New York in the late 'fifties, I interpreted the pressure brought to bear on London from Washington to join the EEC as an indication that the State Department was some 180 years behind the times – it was still fighting the War of Independence. Next to the containment of Communist-Imperialist expansion, the chief object of American foreign policy was to complete the disintegration of the British Empire.

Having shaken off British overlordship two centuries ago, Americans felt and still feel sentimentally committed to encouraging if not actively helping every country that wanted to follow their example. They also favoured any weakening of the special relationship between Britain and the independent countries of the Commonwealth. The most effective means to that end was to push Britain into the Common Market, which would mean the end of Commonwealth Preference. That the United States failed so far to achieve this end was largely due to General de Gaulle's veto.

In the meantime, however, American enthusiasm for Britain's entry into the Common Market has declined quite distinctly. This is due in part to the evidence that even without Britain the EEC has now become a viable and strong economic and political unit. Indeed the increase in the financial strength of Western Europe has exceeded all expectations, while at the same time the financial strength of the United States has declined considerably.

What is more important, it has come to be realised in the United States that the Common Agricultural Policy of the EEC tends to work out very much to the detriment of the American farmer. American industries, too, are beginning to feel the adverse effect of economic integration in Western Europe. It stands to reason that the disadvantages arising for America from the progress towards Western European economic integration would increase considerably if Britain joined the Common Market.

In any case, the rapid progress towards the liquidation of the British Empire has made it appear unnecessary from an

American point of view to favour an acceleration of the process by inducing Britain to sever her Commonwealth links for the sake of joining the Common Market. Indeed second thoughts have come to prevail in Washington as to whether it was, after all, in accordance with the true interests of the United States that British colonies should become independent. Some of these new countries have come to a varying degree under the influence of Moscow or Peking, and a further weakening of their relationship with Britain would naturally strengthen that influence. As for the former Dominions, they have already drifted towards the United States and away from Britain to such an extent that from an American point of view the relative importance of their complete detachment from Britain has declined considerably.

There is good reason for believing that the revival of the trend towards American economic isolationism has been largely the result of the progress towards Western European integration. So long as Western Europe was weak, the United States abstained from adopting policies that were liable to aggravate its weakness. But as economic difficulties in the United States increased and as Western Europe has been gathering strength, it has come to be felt increasingly in Washington that the time has arrived for concentrating on direct American economic interests. It was also felt increasingly in Washington that the bolstering-up of Britain should be henceforth the responsibility of Western Europe and not of the United States, which now has both her hands full, having to cope with her own difficulties, to have time and resources to spare for coping with those of Britain.

The tendency towards American economic isolationism is well on its way towards leading to a trade war between Western Europe and the United States. After having been firm allies in both the economic and political sense, Britain might well find herself fighting an economic war with the United States. Should Britain join a French-dominated Common Market, the anti-American attitude of France would increase the bitterness of the fight, and it might go a long way towards influencing American political attitudes towards Europe.

The likelihood of a trade war with the United States – and, for that matter, with many other countries – has been greatly increased by the finalisation of the Common Agricultural Policy on lines favoured by France. Under that policy farm prices in the EEC will be bolstered up at an artificially high level by means of purchases financed out of a common fund. The artificially high prices are certain to stimulate the increase of agricultural output, and the increasing quantities of land products bought by the common fund will be dumped on markets outside the EEC. Such flagrant aggressive dumping is bound to lead to retaliatory action and will generate much ill-feeling between the agricultural countries affected by it and the Common Market. Britain would have her full share in the adverse economic and political consequences of joining the Common Market. A trade war in which Britain and America would be opponents might be sufficient to end effectively her special relationship with the United States, and also with Canada, Australia, New Zealand and other important countries, the interests of which would be identical with those of the United States.

There is a school of thought in the United States according to which technological progress has made it unnecessary for the defence of the United States to maintain large forces in Europe. As already pointed out in Chapter 2, inter-continental rockets, nuclear submarines and spacecraft have changed basic concepts of global strategy. France's flirtation with the Soviet Union, the East–West *rapprochement* by West Germany under the Brandt Government and the growing influence of Communism in Italy made some quarters in Washington wonder to what extent Western Europe could be depended upon if and when it came to a showdown with the Communist bloc. No such doubts are entertained as far as Britain is concerned. But if she were to tighten her economic and political links with Western Europe, such doubts might well arise and the two Anglo-Saxon countries would drift further apart.

It may well be asked whether it would be really wise to base Britain's security and survival on her dubious relationship with

Western Europe instead of continuing to base it on what is left of the special relationship between the English-speaking peoples. Much more is at stake than relative advantages and disadvantages from the point of view of foreign trade and economic growth – though even from those points of view the balance of argument is distinctly against joining the Common Market. But even if the economic case for joining the Common Market were unanswerable, it would be to Britain's interests to strengthen her links with the United States rather than weaken them for the sake of such economic advantages as she might achieve at that cost.

This aspect of the problem, together with the effect on the Commonwealth discussed in the last chapter, deserves far more attention than arguments based on trade statistics – which in any case relate to the past and do not forecast unpredictable future effects – and on emotional Europeanism which is largely at the root of the agitation in favour of rushing into the Common Market regardless of costs.

The intention of the United States Congress to revert to protectionism in order to improve the balance of payments gave rise to threats of retaliation on the part of the EEC, even though its members owe their recovery after the war, and their resulting present prosperity, to a very large extent to Marshall Aid and to other forms of American assistance, quite apart from their indebtedness for their liberation and for the shield provided by the American military presence in Europe and by the American nuclear deterrent safeguarding them from becoming the victims of Communist Imperialism. That danger is still very much in existence, and the practical wisdom of trying to prevent the United States from recovering her former financial power by means of improving her balance of payments is very much open to question.

Whatever one may think of the attitude of the EEC towards the projected American measures to reduce imports from the EEC and Britain, British retaliation would be quite unpardonable. When sterling was subject to frequent attacks the United States, together with other countries, showed a great deal of understanding towards Britain's imperative need for protecting her balance of payments by discouraging excessive imports. There were no retaliatory measures by countries that were affected by various British protectionist measures or by the devaluation of sterling in 1967. Surely the least the United States is entitled to expect of Britain is that she show the same degree of understanding now that the dollar is in need of reinforcement by protectionist measures.

Having benefited by Lend-Lease during the war, by the big American loan in 1946, by Marshall Aid and other forms of American assistance throughout the post-war period, and especially by the frequent credit and swap facilities obtained from the Federal Reserve on each occasion on which sterling was subject to pressure, the least Britain may reasonably be expected to do is not to try to prevent the United States from defending the dollar now that it is the dollar that is coming under a cloud. Even if Britain is not in a position at present to reciprocate in the form of large-scale financial assistance, she should be willing to accept the unfavourable consequences of the proposed American protectionist measures.

Unfortunately, by threatening with reprisals and by pressing forward with the negotiations for joining the enemy's camp, Britain is behaving with the same short-sighted ingratitude as the EEC countries. Even if gratitude is a rare commodity in politics, it would be in accordance not only with the moral duty of Western European countries but also with their vital interests to do their utmost to help the dollar and the United States.

France under de Gaulle did its utmost to give the EEC the character of an anti-American alliance, and it is because the EEC is incapable of saying 'no' to any French demand that its policy is still anti-American. While it is understandable that any advanced European country should resent the American industrial invasion financed by European capital, there are means of checking it without resorting to policies which are doomed to split the free world into two hostile camps.

Britain should not miss the opportunity of restoring her

former special relationship with the United States by dissociating herself from any EEC reprisals against American protectionist measures. Deplorable as the revival of isolationism in the United States may be, it is a matter of elementary statesmanship to meet it in a spirit of understanding. Britain should show that the Anglo-Saxon special relationship works both ways. By being willing to put up with the disadvantages of the American protectionist measures in the same way in which the United States was willing to put up with British protectionist measures when they were adopted to defend sterling, Britain could and should earn her moral right to depend once more on American assistance when she needs it again and when America is once more in a position to give it. By displaying the same lack of understanding towards the present difficulties of the United States as the EEC countries do, Britain would forfeit her chances of ever benefiting again by generous American assistance in time of need.

Of course any gesture dissociating Britain from reprisals against the United States by the EEC would be detrimental to the progress of the Brussels negotiations. It would revive suspicions that in her heart of hearts Britain is still Anglo-Saxon rather than European. But sooner or later the Continent would have good reason for being grateful to Britain for inducing the United States not to turn her back on Europe.

CHAPTER SIXTEEN

Britain Might Be Unable to Join

VIEWED from a perspective of history, General de Gaulle might well deserve to be regarded as the saviour and patron-saint of Britain, because he saved her from making the biggest mistake in her history. But he is no longer alive and cannot continue to save us from our own folly. Quite conceivably his influence on his former party and on the successor he had appointed might decline in the course of time, and with it would decline the rigidity of French resistance to Britain's admission. Even so, it is advisable to envisage the possibility of a breakdown in the negotiations between Britain and the Common Market. Where would that leave us?

Up to the time of writing very little has transpired about the conditions which the EEC considers the minimum and those which Britain considers the maximum. At an early stage of most negotiations the gap is wide and is gradually narrowed by mutual concessions. It seems that the main point, or one of the main points, around which the battle will rage will be the length of the transition period. It is suggested that the EEC negotiators want it to be as short as three years while the British negotiators hold out for six years, at any rate as far as the application of the Common Agricultural Policy is concerned. There is disagreement also in respect of timing the adjustment of customs barriers to the system that is in operation in the EEC and especially in respect of the terms that would determine the costs of joining the EEC.

Of course it would be very important for Britain not to undertake to apply too suddenly fundamental changes which developed between the EEC countries very gradually over a period of twelve years. It would be a matter of elementary common sense to mitigate the shock by a gradual application of the rules elaborated by the Common Market. But it is at least equally important to reach agreement with the EEC negotiators that to some extent the permanent rules should be adapted to British requirements.

Many enthusiasts of the Common Market idea might feel tempted to sign on the dotted line of the Rome Treaty provided that the changes are not applied in full immediately. The longer the agreed transition period were allowed to continue, the more tempting would it be to accept the grave permanent disadvantages arising from the eventual full application of the EEC rules. After all, six years, or even three years, is a long period. The immediate application of the Common Agricultural Policy would probably be considered quite unacceptable, but if the full cost of joining need not be paid for some time, it may appear to be tempting to accept it for the sake of reaching agreement. Indeed it looks as if the Government might be willing to water down even its claims for special treatment for New Zealand butter and West Indian sugar after the end of the transition period.

A relatively long transition period might be conceded by the EEC for the sake of the willingness of the British negotiators to meet their demands regarding acceptance of the existing rules, because the gradualness of their application might then be regarded by Britain as acceptable. Strong medicine is often prescribed to be taken in small doses. At the end of the transition period the burden assumed by Britain would be just as heavy, but its gradual assumption might encounter less resistance.

The fact that at the annual conference of the Conservative Party in October 1970 only one-third of the delegates voted for rejecting the idea of joining the Common Market outright, while two-thirds were in favour of joining provided that the terms were acceptable, shows the importance of the ability of the British negotiators to obtain concessions. There is bound to be some very hard bargaining. The Government is fully aware that the Party Conference did not give it a blank cheque, and that acceptance of unpopular terms might have repercussions on the domestic political front.

In any case it may safely be taken for granted that the Labour Party will exploit to the full extent the unpopularity of any terms which the Conservative Government would find acceptable. Even before it was known how far the Government was prepared to go, there was a growing agitation by Socialists and trade union leaders against the terms on which Britain was to be admitted. Like Charles James Fox on one occasion, they did not know what the Government's policy was but they declared themselves opposed to it. Once the Government committed itself to terms acceptable to the EEC, the official Opposition is likely to come out against them, declaring that a Labour Government would never agree to join the Common Market on such terms, whatever they may be. Indeed Mr Wilson, knowing only too well on which side his political bread is buttered, might even go as far as to declare that an agreement on such terms would be repudiated by the next Labour Government.

Any such declaration might be sufficient to torpedo the negotiations, not only because Mr Heath would have no desire to commit political suicide but also because the EEC Governments would not want to disorganise their well-established system for the sake of admitting Britain temporarily until the next General Election. Their negotiators might insist on a bipartisan policy that would ensure that the whole house of cards did not collapse after a change of Government.

The Labour Party, for its part, would have none of that. It would be reluctant to forgo the political advantages it would stand to gain as a result of the unpopularity of the agreement or of certain of its terms. In such circumstances Britain's application for membership of the EEC might well fail once more. Possibly even the Government itself would not be prepared to go far enough to satisfy the EEC.

But it is bound to take some time before this stage would be reached and before it would be admitted in public that the negotiations have broken down. It may take at least a year, perhaps two or even three years, during which the possibility that Britain would join would continue to exist. Even if it should become evident that the negotiations are not going well, the possibility of an eventual compromise could not be ruled out. It very often happens in the course of long and difficult international negotiations that, just when the parties are on the point of giving up, an eleventh-hour effort to avoid a deadlock leads to an unexpected settlement. The ever-present possibility of this means that for something like two or three years all the interested parties in Britain or abroad would be kept in uncertainty about their prospects. Although this aspect of the subject was touched upon earlier, it deserves more detailed treatment.

Nobody would be able to base their plans on the certain knowledge that Britain would be in the Common Market or on the certainty that she would stay out of it. Yet it may be of considerable importance from the point of view of planning industrial or agricultural investment whether in two or three years' time Britain begins to apply the EEC rules. Some industries and some types of agricultural production would stand to benefit by Britain's entry, so that it would be to the interests of those concerned to increase their productive capacity. On the other hand, Britain's entry would be necessarily detrimental to certain industries and certain lines of agricultural production, so that it would be to the interests of those concerned to reduce their capacity or to close down altogether. But in order to take such decisions they would have to know for certain that the negotiations would end in an agreement, and they would have to have an idea of the kind of agreement that is likely to emerge. But even the Government itself is not in a position to know and it would not be in a position to give private interests any useful guidance.

The same is true concerning producers in the Commonwealth and elsewhere who are interested in the British markets. They will have no means of knowing whether to prepare themselves for a considerable reduction of their competitive capacity in Britain as a result of the changes in the customs system brought about by her membership of the Common Market. But in view of the British Government's oft-expressed determination to join the EEC, a great many of the producers in the Commonwealth and elsewhere are liable to prefer to be on the safe side and to make their arrangements on the assumption that in a few years they would lose the whole or part of their present British markets. They would be inclined to reorientate their exports towards other markets and to adapt their production to the requirements of those markets or of their domestic markets. Importers, too, might look round for alternative suppliers at home or abroad. Their Governments, too, might be inclined to conclude trade agreements to assist the reorientation of the foreign trade of their nationals. They might join other trading areas, or they might take other measures to divert trade from Britain while the going is good, so as to mitigate the shock if and when Britain joins the Common Market.

This means that, long before the outcome of the talks becomes evident, British exporters are liable to lose markets in the Commonwealth and in other countries outside the EEC. Should the negotiations break down, British exporters and the Government would be faced by the task of having to recover such lost markets, which would not be easy in many instances. Some markets might be lost irretrievably. For instance, should the plan of a Pacific trading area between Japan, Australia, New Zealand and other countries materialise during the course of the British negotiations with the EEC, British goods in those countries might be replaced by Japanese goods which have in any case the advantage of lower transport costs.

In the last chapter we referred to the protectionist trend that is developing in the United States, largely as a result of the progress of European economic integration. Anticipation of an escalation of that progress as a result of an eventual successful conclusion of the negotiation between Britain and the EEC will tend to strengthen the protectionist lobbies in Washington. Even if retaliatory measures should lead to a contraction of the British markets for American goods, American protectionists are in a position to argue that such contraction would take place in any case once Britain has joined the Common Market.

It is conceivable that, if in 1972 or 1973 the Government should be impelled to admit the failure of its endeavours to join the Common Market, Britain would find herself in a position in which she would get the worst of all worlds. By that time her former non-European trading partners would have made their arrangements in anticipation of the effects of British membership of the Common Market. I am not suggesting that in most cases it would be impossible to turn a new leaf and regain ground unnecessarily lost. But it might prove to be up-hill work. For this reason it would be a matter of elementary statesmanship not to drag out the negotiations once it becomes evident that no agreement would be possible on terms acceptable to Britain, and especially not to drag them out because of sheer reluctance to concede failure.

The sooner it is known whether Britain would be able to join or not, the better for everybody concerned. Yet even before the negotiations were opened it was stated that they would last something like two years. Would it really be necessary to go through the gestures of protracted negotiations in order that the Government should feel satisfied, and should satisfy its pro-common Market supporters, that it 'left no stones unturned' and that it 'explored every avenue'? Or that it should satisfy opponents of joining the EEC that it put up a really tough fight before conceding terms which, however unsatisfactory, were the only ones on which agreement was at all possible? Much more important considerations are at stake.

CHAPTER SEVENTEEN

An Atlantic Free Trade Area?

THROUGHOUT this book the proposal to join the Common Market has been subject to criticism from a wide variety of points of view. The time has now arrived to explore some of the alternative solutions.

Of course the obvious alternative would be simply *not* to join the Common Market and carry on under the existing system. This solution might impose itself on Britain whether she likes it or not, if the Brussels negotiations should break down once more. In the absence of any other arrangement the system of Commonwealth Preference and EFTA would presumably continue, even though, as already pointed out, both might be weakened under the influence of the uncertainty created by the prolonged negotiations with the EEC. For our present trading partners in EFTA and in the Commonwealth, envisaging the likelihood of a success of our negotiations, might make their own arrangements, to the permanent detriment of their trade with Britain.

But there are alternatives to joining the Common Market other than merely maintaining the *status quo*. It is essential that British public opinion should be made fully aware of their existence, so as to counteract the widespread feeling, spread successfully by pro-Common Market propaganda, that Britain simply must accept the best terms obtainable at Brussels, whatever those terms may be. It is also essential that the EEC Governments should be made aware of the existence of these alternatives. This is also to the interests even of those in favour of joining the Common Market. For, as a result of the realisation in Brussels of the existence of acceptable alternatives, the EEC negotiators might take a less uncompromising line and might drive a less hard bargain, so that the chances of a settlement might consequently improve.

The most obvious alternative would be the extension of EFTA to include the Commonwealth – that is to say, those countries of the Commonwealth which are willing to participate. It seems probable that, faced with the alternative of losing their British markets as a result of Britain's adherence to the Common Market, quite a number of Commonwealth countries would be willing and even eager to adopt the solution of replacing Commonwealth Preference by membership in a free trade area. A number of other Commonwealth countries, while unwilling to do away altogether with customs barriers against goods from Britain and from other countries of the proposed free trade area, might be willing to become associates on special terms.

Needless to say, from a British point of view many of the arguments used against joining the Common Market would also apply against the above formula. For instance, imports from Canada, Australia and also from countries with less highly developed industries using cheap labour would be able to compete successfully with British industries in the British domestic market in respect of a wide variety of goods. Some British firms or industries would be certain to be losers on balance, while others would stand to gain through the free admission of their goods to countries in which they are at present subject to preferential duties. However, from a general point of view the losses of British firms would not be the gains of foreign firms but the gains of Commonwealth firms. The money would remain, so to say, in the family. As far as countries which use cheap labour are concerned, they are already dangerous competitors in textiles and many other lines, and the difference resulting from a complete abolition of the low preferential duties would be a mere matter of degree.

Needless to say, the expansion of the market to which British goods could be sold free of customs barriers would not in itself solve all our problems any more than joining the Common Market would solve them, and it would create quite a number of new problems. Nevertheless, from an economic point of view it would be a solution that would be preferable to the EEC solution.

The association of the United Kingdom and the countries of EFTA with the Commonwealth would be a more natural combination of countries than the association with highly industrialised Western Europe. It would not lead to a rise in food prices. It would not involve heavy financial sacrifices. It would not call for complicated changes necessitated by the higher degree of economic integration with the EEC.

From a political point of view it would give the Commonwealth a new lease of life. First of all, it would obviate the necessity for sacrificing our close relationship with the former Dominions. We would in fact reinforce not only our trade links but also our political and psychological links. The voluntary restraint on the export of capital to Australia and New Zealand would have to be removed, so as to provide every opportunity for British capital and enterprise to take the lion's share in the development of their natural resources. In spite of having drifted apart to some extent in recent years, those countries, and a number of others, are still essentially British in sentiment. Their progress with our assistance would greatly strengthen these sentiments. Britain would have close connections with important and expanding countries in the Pacific and elsewhere, on which she would be able to depend in good times and in bad times – which is more than could be said about some of our partners in an enlarged EEC.

If handled in the right way, a restoration of Commonwealth ties at a moment when they were in danger of being severed might well generate a badly needed spirit of national regeneration at home. British people should be made to realise that this revival would justify once more the adjective 'Great' before 'Britain' in fact and not only in name, that it would give them a chance to recover national greatness. To be once more the centre of a far-flung Empire – I use the term in its geographical and not its political sense – would be something to be proud of, however much such sentiments may be denigrated by Little

Englanders. Perhaps a realisation of greatness regained might revive the true British spirit which had built the Empire and maintained it over centuries. It might provide the desperately needed antidote to the poison of short-sighted greed and unintelligent selfishness which is to blame for most of Britain's troubles in recent years. In other words, it might cure the 'English disease'

The reversal of the trend towards a disintegration of the Commonwealth would go a long way towards restoring the self-respect of the British people and the respect of other nations. Although a relatively small number of people have been capable of working themselves into fanatical enthusiasm about the idea of a united Western Europe, I doubt if it can possibly have anything like the same emotional appeal to the British people as a whole as a revival of the Commonwealth and of British greatness. Should the widespread realisation of the immense opportunities in Australia and elsewhere provide inspiration for making a supreme effort to take advantage of it, Britain would become once more a strong and proud country and sterling might become once more a strong and proud currency.

But the British Conservative Government seems to have no interest in restoring national greatness. Indeed, to curry favour in Brussels by showing that it is 100 per cent European and has no use for the tens of millions of people of British stock who reside outside Europe, it hastened to impose duties on food imported from the Commonwealth even before it was certain that the negotiations would lead to an acceptable agreement. One of the results of this ill-advised step will be that the terms of the agreement will be less favourable to Britain, because this subservient gesture is bound to toughen the EEC's attitude.

It seems that nothing short of a miracle could save Britain from the irreparable consequences of jettisoning the Commonwealth. But miracles do occur even in the twentieth century. I refuse to abandon hope until the deed is done, that common sense might yet prevail, and the Commonwealth might be saved.

A revival of the moribund Sterling Area would accompany the revival of the Commonwealth. This would be a result for the sake of which it would be well worth while to put up with the disadvantages that inevitably accompany a major change. Many individuals would be affected unfavourably, but they would stand a better chance of sharing eventually in the beneficial effects of the change in other spheres.

Another alternative to joining the EEC is the creation of the widely favoured Atlantic Free Trade Area. It has been advocated in many quarters in this country during recent years and has an extensive literature both over here and, to a lesser extent, in Canada and the United States. It would mean an extension of EFTA to cover North America, with or without the inclusion of Commonwealth countries apart from Canada. The inclusion of Japan is also suggested by some advocates of this solution. But even without going beyond EFTA and North America, it would provide a trading area the capacity of which would exceed very considerably that of the EEC.

The basic idea of this solution, too, should appeal to the imagination. It would mean that Anglo-Saxon countries would be included in the same trading area and that trade barriers between English-speaking nations would be eliminated. After all, the link of language, and that of identical or nearly identical cultural and historical heritage, does count for something even in an increasingly materialistic world. Even if Britain should inevitably play the part of the junior partner in this economic world Empire which would surpass any other conceivable trading area, its role would compare favourably with the role it would play in an economically and possibly politically integrated Western Europe.

Needless to say, the removal of customs barriers would let loose a flood of American goods on to the British market and this would lead to some painful readjustments, possibly in some respects even more painful than the free admission of Western European manufactured goods. But the almost inevitable Americanisation of a large part of British industries would make for a much higher degree of efficiency than any that is likely to be achieved under the impact of Britain's admission into the Common Market. Those who believe in the all-curing effect of competition, of a wide market and of large units should prefer, in order to be consistent, the North American solution to the Western European solution.

The main snag is that the United States would in all probability reject the idea. The American trend at the time of writing is towards isolationism. There would be a sufficiently large number of American industries which would expect to be affected unfavourably by the removal of customs barriers against British imports to mobilise powerful political influences against the scheme. Yet on the other hand American agriculture is now threatened with the loss of the British market if we should join the EEC. If the agricultural lobby, together with the lobbies of American exporting industries which would stand to gain, were to throw their influence into the scale, their aggregate weight might conceivably counterbalance the aggregate weight of influence in the opposite sense. Anyhow, a serious attempt by Britain to bridge the widening gap between the two Anglo-Saxon nations would go some way towards strengthening the special relationship with the United States even if it were doomed to end in failure.

As far as Canada is concerned, she stands to lose even more than the United States through the inclusion of Britain in the Common Market. There could be, moreover, little doubt that a relative increase of British economic influence in Canada, offsetting to some extent the increasingly one-sided and overwhelmingly American influence, would be welcomed. From a British point of view it would be infinitely preferable if a substantial part of the Commonwealth in addition to Canada were also included. Australia and New Zealand in particular would be certain to join with enthusiasm such an extended arrangement. From a political and military point of view they are already in the American sphere of influence. I am sure there are no Australian or New Zealanders who would not prefer to belong to a joint Anglo-American sphere of influence.

Yet another alternative would be a free trade area to embrace the entire free world. That was the ultimate ideal which GATT and the Kennedy Rounds aimed at approaching if not actually attaining. While world economic integration may be sheer Utopia, world free trade is not entirely beyond the realm of possibility – though perhaps not in the lifetime of the present generation. Possibly the best way of approaching that goal might be through the intermediary of regional free trade areas such as the EEC, EFTA, NAFTA, a Pacific Free Trade Area and a Latin American Free Trade Area with or without advanced economic integration. Perhaps it might be easier to negotiate agreements for integration between a small number of large trading areas.

However, it would be wishful thinking to assess the possibilities of world-wide free trade or even of free trade in the free world as high. Less ambitious projects – whether in the sense of being confined to a more limited geographical area or in the sense of necessitating a smaller degree of economic and political integration – stand a better chance of becoming reality.

But even if every attempt should fail and if free trade for Britain should remain confined to EFTA and, subject to lowered customs barriers, to the Commonwealth, that in itself would not prevent accelerated growth and rise in the standard of living. What really matters is willingness to work, under a system that encourages efficient management instead of discouraging it. A hard-working and efficiently managed community could live and prosper increasingly even in a desert which it could convert into a flourishing country, provided that its members are interested not only in what they could get out of the community but also in what they give the community.

So long as the British nation was the finest nation in world history, most countries of the British Empire gladly remained members of that association of nations. It was mainly the deterioration of the British character since the end of the Second World War that stimulated movements to break away from a country which was no longer able to play its former part in aiding and inspiring progress all over the five continents. If Britain were still at her best she would be welcomed with open arms in the Common Market and in any other association of nations. She would not have to beg for admission cap in hand but could walk in with her head erect, laying down the terms on which she is prepared to join instead of awaiting the decision of other nations about the terms on which they might graciously consent to admit her. One of our terms should be that France must rejoin NATO and abandon her anti-American policy before Britain would want to have closer association with her.

It would be infinitely more dignified if, instead of begging for admittance in the mistaken hope that it would cure her troubles, Britain were to cure her troubles first, so as to be in a position to negotiate from strength instead of negotiating from weakness. It would then be possible to obtain admission on terms which would not mean jettisoning the loyal countries of the Commonwealth or bringing the English-speaking nations into conflict with each other. Also, if Britain were in a position to join the Common Market from a position of strength, so that she would constitute an asset and not a liability, she might make her influence felt to a sufficient degree to hold integrated Western Europe together. It would be one thing for the Western European nations to be in close association with an economically stable and militarily powerful Britain that may safely rely on the economic, political and military support of Commonwealth countries and of the United States. It would be a totally different thing for them to admit reluctantly a weakened and economically unstable Britain that has already reduced her contacts with all overseas English-speaking nations. No wonder in existing circumstances Paris and Brussels are convinced that they can dictate the terms.

To make the EEC realise that they do not hold all the trumps, the British Government should embark on negotiations for alternative solutions to that of joining the Common Market. At the same time Britain's bargaining position should be strengthened by making a supreme effort to restore Britain's lost power and prestige. A beginning to that end has already been made by the new Government by a display of firmness in an effort to restore discipline, which is a preliminary condition of recovering national greatness. If only the Government insisted in Brussels on terms more acceptable to Britain – its initial offer, by agreeing to include agriculture and by agreeing that after the period of transition the concessions for the benefit of some Commonwealth countries would cease, has gone much too far towards sacrificing British interests – an acceptable agreement might possibly be reached. If not, one of the preferable alternatives should be chosen. No agreement would be infinitely preferable to a bad agreement.

Perhaps the British public, by showing that it has more sense than its leaders, might yet make the latter realise that their choice of a fatally ill-advised solution would amount to political suicide. But judging by the speeding-up of the discussions in Brussels, and by the hasty adoption of food import duties in advance of any agreement, it seems highly probable that Britain is doomed to throw in her lot with Western Europe. Alternative solutions are not even considered.

There is still a possibility that some miracle might save Britain from the disastrous consequences of the short-sightedness and dogmatism of her politicians. I cannot help hoping that Mr. Heath might realise before it is too late that the 'silent majority' – on whose support the success of his tenure of office depends – is decidedly against joining the Common Market. He could ill afford to antagonise them. And I have not given up hope that, as a good democrat, he will respect the the wishes of the nation.

Index